FAMILIES AND FRIENDS

How to help your child form happy relationships

Dr John Pearce

Thorsons
An Imprint of HarperCollinsPublishers

Thorsons
An Imprint of Grafton Books
A Division of HarperCollins*Publishers*
77-85 Fulham Palace Road,
Hammersmith, London W6 8JB

Published by Thorsons 1991

1 3 5 7 9 10 8 6 4 2

British Library Cataloguing in Publication Data

Pearce, John *1940 Oct. 27–*
Families and friends: how to help your child form happy
relationships.
1. Children. Interpersonal relationships with families
I. Title
646.78

ISBN 0 7225 1725 4

Typeset by Harper Phototypesetters Limited,
Northampton, England

Printed and bound in Great Britain by
Collins Manufacturing, Glasgow

To My Family

CONTENTS

INTRODUCTION

What is the point of families? They cause arguments, make people upset, and sometimes even break down altogether, leaving the children distressed and confused. Families provide love and caring that is just as vital to children's development as food is. We all need the nourishment, but too much or too little food can be bad for the health, and in the same way overprotective or neglectful families may lead to emotional ill health.

Unfortunately the importance of the family is often underestimated. It isn't unusual to hear people say that families are not that important – we can get by without them. People quote the example of successful single parents, foster parents, the kibbutz and cultures where children are brought up as part of a large community.

There is no doubt that children can be cared for quite adequately without having to be in a 'normal' two parent family. It isn't difficult to believe that children might be better off without a 'normal' family if the parents always argue with each other or are unable to care adequately for their children. If you are a single parent, family relationships may be easier to cope with in some ways because there is only one adult, but this can make the parent–child relationship all the more intense and difficult to manage.

Families are often held responsible for most of the problems of society and of course this means that the blame falls

on the parents. Parents have a really tough time! Mothers
are expected to be Supermums as well as housekeepers and
wage earners. Fathers must earn a reasonable wage and at
the same time they must be Superdads, and DIY specialists.
If this wasn't enough each parent is also expected to be able
to do everything that the other does. Such high expectations, so much to do and so little time to do it in!

There is no job that is more important and vital to the
future of our society than being a parent, and yet parenting
is not fully valued by society. Unlike people in business,
sports, and entertainment, parents and others involved in
childcare are not given high status or paid well for the
difficult job that they do. The qualities of good parenting,
such as continuity of care, consistency, and responsiveness
to children's needs don't seem to be given the high value
that they deserve.

This book recognizes the overriding importance of parenting skills to protect the future of our children and our world. It is written specially for parents who wish to know more about family relationships and how to survive them without feeling either too guilty, distressed, or too exhausted.

Over the past few years there have been great advances in the understanding of how things go wrong in families and what can be done about it. But childcare is so easily influenced by fashions that parents often follow the latest trend without knowing what evidence there is to back it up. Unfortunately, the complete information on family relationships isn't easily available because research is published in so many different scientific journals and even then the research is sometimes contradictory. I have tried to give some clear and practical guidelines about some of the common problems that occur in family relationships and how to cope with them.

Don't worry too much if you find it difficult to cope with your family – at least you are in good company because most people feel the same at one time or another. However, there are many things that can be done to make family life go along more smoothly and you should find most aspects covered here. The book is mainly about 'normal' relationships and day-to-day problems that are not a major concern. Nevertheless these daily hassles may take up a lot of your time and energy and could even build up into big problems if allowed to continue. Many of the relationship problems that we have as adults can be traced back to our childhood experiences so it is best to sort things out early on rather than to just hope for the best.

You might ask, 'Why do parents need to read a book on family relationships? Surely we are all different and each family is best at deciding how it wants to function?' This approach certainly works for some lucky families, but many parents have to struggle all the time to get family life running well and often feel confused about what is the best approach. More parents than ever before have to cope with the care of their children on their own (about 1 in 12 families at the last count). Also more families have both parents going out to work (about 60 per cent of families with school age children). Both these factors make life more complicated for parents and give less time and energy for working out how to solve any problems that do occur.

You may think that I sometimes take a rather firm line that could cause children or parents to become upset, but if you read the book carefully you will find there is always a good reason for being tough. Please remember that being loving and being indulgent are not the same thing. Indeed, more trouble is caused by parents giving in 'for a quiet life' than for any other reason. It is not all that easy to stick to what you have said and to keep to what you believe is right, especially if you are not sure that you are doing the right thing in the first place. Children gain a great deal of security and comfort when their parents are prepared to be firm and give clear limits to their behaviour in a consistent and caring way. In fact this is a good way of showing your love for your child.

I would like you to feel that I am talking directly to you as you read through the book. You can 'talk' back to me if you don't agree with what I have said or if you don't understand. Then read on and it should become clear why I have taken a certain line rather than any other. Don't hold back from having an argument with me in your head or asking someone else what they think. In this way you will become much clearer about what you believe yourself.

Childcare is not so much about right and wrong, but more about finding the best compromise between the various demands of family life. For this reason it is impossible to 'get it right' all the time and this often leads to feelings of guilt. In fact, a normal part of being a parent is feeling guilty about not always doing the right thing for your child!

If you are unsure about your own ideas, but have some reservations about what I have written. I would like you to follow my suggestions as closely as possible, in spite of any reservations you might have. I have been very careful to give guidelines and advice only where I am confident that it is safe, reasonable, and effective. If you have followed the guidelines carefully and they have still not worked, please don't immediately think that I have got it all wrong. It is much more likely that you haven't been sticking closely enough to what I have said. So read the book again, have another go . . . and don't give up!

It is the love you have for your child that makes being a parent so fulfilling and full of joy. But it is the same bond of affection that makes it so painful and distressing when things go wrong. Our feelings of love vary from time to time and fortunately it isn't necessary to love your child all the time in order to be a reasonable parent.

At the end of the book there is a section outlining some of the research on family life for those of you who would like to have more detail and to read further on the subject. I hope that there is something to interest everyone, even if you have no children. You might even find out something about yourself and the reasons for your own relationship hang-ups which can almost always be traced back to childhood.

CHAPTER 1

MAKING
A HAPPY FAMILY

Bonding – Sticking Together

From the moment of conception the making of a family has started. As soon as a couple know about the pregnancy, the process of 'bonding' to the baby starts. Bonding is a bit like emotional glue! It is the stuff that holds relationships together and it is stronger than just affection alone. You can see the powerful effects of the bonding in a mother's feelings of love and caring if her child is ill or upset.

The real power of bonding is seen at its strongest when a relationship is broken, for example when someone close to you dies or if a marriage breaks down. The emotional pain that is caused by breaking a bonded relationship helps to protect relationships and keep them going, especially between parents and their child.

The bonding of the mother and father to their child grows stronger as the pregnancy progresses. Naturally, it is the mother who usually feels closest to the baby because she is so intimately involved, but there is nothing wrong with a father having feelings of bonding to the unborn child that are just as strong or maybe even stronger than those of the mother. Hearing the baby's heart beat either with a stethoscope or by the father listening directly to the mother's tummy can be very exciting and increase the bonding still further at an early stage in the development of the child. The bonding process continues and reaches a peak around the time of birth. The first few days after birth have been found to be particularly important for the bonding of a mother to her child. This is why early contact between mother and child is always encouraged.

The parent–child bond continues to grow stronger over the first few years, but later on the closeness of the bonding has to be loosened so that the child can become independent without this being too painful. Even when children are finally grown up, the emotional bond that parents feel for their child continues.

One of the most delicate and skilful things that a parent has to do is to keep the bond with their child balanced so that it is neither too close nor too distant. The closeness has to be continually adjusted and there will be many times when parents have to go against their natural instincts to allow their child to do things independently – for example, when children start at school or stay away from home on their own for the first time. The strong distressing feelings that occur at these times often take parents by surprise.

Of course it isn't only parents and children who can form a close bonded relationship. Adults can also bond to each other as in a marriage or friendship. The ability of parents to form a bond with each other depends to a large extent on how well they were bonded to their own parents as a child. Parents who have had strong bonds with their parents when they were children will usually find it easy to keep good relationships going as adults. However, even if one parent has had a difficulty bonding and had an unsettled time as a child, these problems can be compensated for by marrying someone who has had a good experience as a child.

Child-Bonding

This bonding between parents and their child is a two-way process, but the attachment of a child to its parents starts very gradually at first and only becomes really obvious round about six months when children show distress and anxiety if they are separated from their parents. Not surprisingly this is called 'separation anxiety'. It is a normal, healthy response, but if the anxiety grows too strong it may cause trouble for a child going off to school or away from home for some other reason.

From around six months old children become steadily more closely bonded to their parents over several years. By the age of about 7 years your child can be expected to have a firm emotional bond to you that will then continue to become more solid over the next few years. The strength of the child–parent bond will depend on a number of different factors such as:

- **The age of the child**
- **The response of the parent to the child**
- **The amount of time the child spends with the parent**
- **The other people who provide care for the child**
- **The emotional atmosphere in which the child is brought up**

It is possible to interfere with a child's bonding by frequent changes of carers, by making the show of love and affection unpredictable or by bringing the child up in an atmosphere of hostility and criticism. If a firm child–parent bond is not made during childhood, then it is quite likely that the child will have difficulty making and keeping relationships as an adult. This may sound rather worrying, but fortunately most children are very resilient and can survive some remarkably unhappy experiences. Here are some factors that can help and protect a child from relationship problems later on even if there have been problems with bonding:

- **The bonding may be to a brother or sister or other relative living at home, such as a grandparent.**
- **Young children will bond quite easily to a foster parent or adoptive parent.**
- **A continuing good relationship with someone outside the family such as a teacher or neighbour can be very helpful.**
- **Even as an adult a close loving relationship can compensate for poor bonding as a child.**

Substitute Parents

The bonding process of the child to a parent is at its strongest over the first few years. This means that if another adult spends a considerable time with a child during this period of active bonding, the child may bond to them rather than the parent. Sometimes this happens between a grandmother and her grandchild if she cares for the child for more time than the parent or if the quality of the relationship is better. This point is worth considering if your mother lives with you and looks after your child while you go to work. Your child could become more closely bonded to her than to you, unless you make a point of spending time with your child in an intimate loving relationship.

It is unlikely that any child would become bonded to a childminder, unless they spend more time with them than with their parents, or the quality of the parent–child relationship is unsatisfactory. Very young children can bond to foster parents, but the process takes many months with little or no contact with the natural parents.

Any child adopted before the age of 4 or 5 is likely to grow up with a deep feeling that their adoptive parents are their natural parents even if they 'know' that this isn't true. Sometimes these conflicting thoughts and feelings can cause adopted children to become quite muddled unless the reality of their strong attachment is recognized. The same feelings of confusion can occur if a step-parent joins the family when the child is still very young. The young child may soon come to feel that the step-parent is a real parent (see Chapter 5 — Alternative Families).

The attachment of a child to a parent is a delicate and complex process and it can be difficult to work out exactly what is happening if the parent–child bonding has been interrupted for any reason. There are three main factors that need to be taken into account:

1. **The time that the child spends with the carer**
2. **The quality of the time spent with the carer**
3. **The stage of development that the child has reached**

The quality of a relationship isn't easy to define or measure, but the table below will give you some idea of the more important qualities that go to make good or bad relationships.

Few if any of us manage to have all the good qualities or avoid the bad ones all the time, and the positive qualities are not unique to parents: this is why it is possible to substitute for parental care. Of course, blood (genetic) relationships are important, but they are not absolutely vital. Most people would agree that the emotional relationship or bonding is even more important.

There are many different ways in which parental care can be substituted for or supplemented by another person or by a group of people. The evidence seems to show that substitute care is unlikely to cause major problems, pro-

Positive Qualities	Negative Qualities
warm and affectionate	cold and hostile
clear limit setting	inconsistent care
quick to recognize needs	unresponsive to needs
accepting of faults	rejecting
predictable and consistent	unpredictable
respecting the individual	disrespectful
recognition of good qualities	emphasis on bad qualities

vided that children continue to experience positive, loving relationships and good child care.

Do We Need Families?

At least 40 per cent of all children experience some form of substitute parenting. This is a very large number of children and is mainly due to family breakdown or death of a parent. A relatively small number of children are fostered or adopted and a similarly small number are brought up mainly in boarding schools and children's homes, or by nannies or grannies. There is evidence that the children who have not experienced continuous care in a two parent family have more problems as adults, but the reasons for this are far from straightforward.

Children who have experienced the breakdown of their family do particularly badly. This is probably largely due to the distressing experiences that the children go through before, during, and after the divorce of their parents (see Chapter 5 Alternative Families). Being brought up in a home that has a lot of negative relationships or experiencing family breakdown seems to cause many more problems for children than not being in a 'normal' two parent family. This is because the important process of bonding and relationship formation can still be compensated for even if there is only one parent.

There are many advantages for children who have a stable family life where the family tasks are shared by a father and mother in much the same way as has occurred for thousands of years. Here are some of the advantages:

- **Mutual support by the parents for each other**
- **Bonding and blood ties are likely to be strong**
- **Male and female role models are available**
- **Mother and father roles complement each other**
- **There may be a better standard of living due to higher income**
- **Easy learning about relationships by observation**

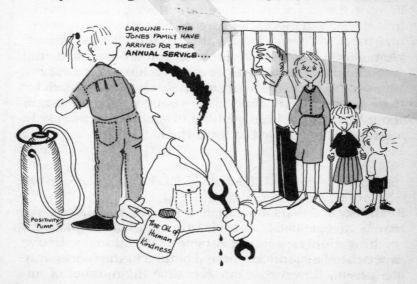

Of course family life isn't always full of peace and light. But this is no reason to condemn families. It would be much the same as saying cars are no good and we should do away with them because they have accidents and break down. Don't forget that what happens to cars depends on how well they are looked after and how carefully they are driven. The same applies to families, but no one has to pass a test before getting into a family!

Families and parents have the most important of all jobs to do – to protect and care for the next generation on which our future depends. The standard two parent family has been shown to be the most effective and efficient unit for the care of children if it is working properly. Strangely our society seems to have little respect for parents and the responsibility involved in bringing up children.

Sadly, anyone who is involved in the direct care of children tends to get little respect, and childcare jobs such as childminder, teacher, or childcare worker don't attract much in the way of financial reward. Having a family results in less time and money for parents. The State fails to recognize the heavy responsibility that parents take on. Parents' views have only just recently begun to be taken into account when planning services for children. Parents have very poor access to the information that is required in order to be a good parent. How many young people are taught about bonding and the qualities of good relationships? In most cases they are left to learn the hard way.

Single Parents

By the age of 5 years more than 10 per cent of children will have been separated from their father or mother and before reaching adulthood almost 50 per cent of children will have experienced a significant period of time in the care of only one parent. However, at any one time the number of unsupported one parent families is not that high (about 5 per cent) because the majority of single parents find a new partner within a short time – although this is more often the case for fathers than for mothers.

Any parent trying to bring up one or more children on their own is attempting something that is going to be difficult. In spite of this there is little difference in a child's ability to bond, whether to one or to two parents. A single parent family can therefore work, but in most cases there are many difficulties stacked up against them. Here are some of the problems that single parents have to cope with, even if they have *chosen* to bring up children in this way:

- **a high rate of poverty**
- **a lower standard of living**
- **a reduced earning capacity**
- **a higher rate of social problems**
- **a high level of dissatisfaction**
- **a higher rate of social isolation**
- **an increased rate of emotional problems for the single parent**
- **an increased rate of behaviour problems in the children**
- **an increased rate of learning problems in the children**

The single parent certainly has a lot of difficulties to cope with. However, the link between being a single parent and having problems is a very complicated one. Many single parents are highly successful in bringing up their children and coping with all the adversity. Indeed, some single parents have an easier time being on their own than, for example, two parents who can't agree or than a family where one parent is ill or disabled. Unfortunately, the problems of bringing up children on your own can easily develop into a vicious self-perpetuating cycle.

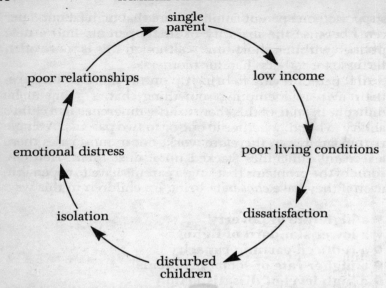

Most single parents are young and in the case of a teenage parent the problems outlined above are all much more serious and both the mother and the child suffer. The majority of children of very young parents have behaviour problems of one sort or another. However, if the extended family is able to support the young parent the outlook is much better.

Family Support

Many of the day-to-day problems of keeping a family going can be helped by having some outside support. Grandparents have considerable power to support, or occasionally to undermine, the family. Neighbours and friends are also helpful and it is a shame that this pool of assistance isn't drawn on more. Our families have tended to become rather isolated and often delay asking for help until things are desperate. Fortunately new voluntary organizations are now being set up to provide this type of help. There is probably one in the area where you live. If not, how about starting one yourself?

All the evidence shows that it is supportive relationships that make families work well. Even parents with rather limited skills and disadvantaged childhood experiences can do well if they have the support of a loving and involved partner. Although a professional person can offer a great deal of support in some cases, it is nothing like as helpful as the help that is always there, ready and available within the network of family and friends.

Making Families Work

Starting a family isn't that difficult, but keeping it going and making it work is another matter. The one to one relationship that a couple have before the arrival of a child is easy to cope with when compared with the four ways of relating after the baby is born, when the relationships are as follows:

mother – child
father   – child
mother – father
father   – child – mother

These four ways of relating include the possibility of each person being excluded from the relationship of the other two and also the possibility of a three-way relationship occurring for the first time. If a second or third child arrives, the complications in family relationships can become quite confusing! More than three children and all kinds of relationship problems occur – especially problems with communication.

... MORE THAN THREE CHILDREN AND **ALL KINDS OF PROBLEMS OCCUR** ....

Good Communication

Good communication is obviously an important part of making a family work well. But many of us are not natural communicators and very young children use rather primitive ways of communicating – such as screaming or being naughty. Children need to be taught how to communicate and parents may need to keep practising to improve their own communication skills. Here are some ideas of ways to help family communication

- **The radio and especially the television make talking to each other very difficult, if not impossible. Turn them off!**
- **Remember that communication takes time. It helps if there are regular times during the day when the family gets together to talk and to let each other know what is happening. Meal times may be convenient, or over a cup of tea.**
- **Children learn about communication from their parents and other adults around them. To be a good communicator you have to be a bit of an actor or actress and remember the following seven points:**

1. Use only a few words
2. Simple words are best
3. Make your facial expression fit what you say
4. The tone of your voice must back up what you say
5. Gestures may also reinforce your words
6. Make sure that you have your child's attention
7. Your child should look you in the face

- Listening is just as important as talking. Most children, and even some adults, need a lot of help in knowing when to keep quiet. Listening is a skill that has to be learnt and needs practice.
- Children often talk a lot and at the same time as other people. You may need to be very tough about controlling who speaks when. It can help if you sometimes get every one to be completely quiet and then give each person time to have their say. It sounds artificial but it works!
- It is a good idea to get children into the habit of communicating regularly about things that don't matter very much. Anything that they are interested in will do. Then they will be able to cope when it is really important that they do communicate and not just go silent.

Time for the Family

Not only is time needed for communication, but time is also needed for all family members just to spend some time together. Being together as a family is increasingly difficult with all the demands of everyday life so special efforts have to be made to make this possible. At least once a day would be a reasonable minimum, or as near to this as possible.

Of course just spending time together isn't enough – it depends what you are doing when you are all together. The most important thing is that you are all enjoying what you are doing. Having meals together is a good way of doing this, but it should be possible to find other things you all like doing (watching the TV together may be enjoyable, but it isn't as good as joining in *doing* something together, such as a game or going for a walk as a family).

So it is the *quality* of the time together that is more important than the *quantity* of time. You could spend days together in the same house but take little notice of each other and live very separate lives. Family time needs to be made special so that everyone respects and values it. This has to be worked at – it won't just happen. You will know when this special family time has been achieved because

EVERYBODY WILL LOOK FORWARD TO THE NEXT TIME YOU ARE **ALL TOGETHER**....

everybody will look forward to the next time you are all together.

Showing Appreciation

Perhaps one of the most annoying things about being together in a family is that it is all too easy to take what everybody does to help the family for granted. Appreciation needs to be shown for quite ordinary things like doing

the housework or earning the money to keep the family going.

Showing appreciation is one way of letting people know that you think that they are good to be with. This in turn will help a parent or child to feel good about themselves. Being appreciated leads to a high self esteem which has been found to be very protective and to make it possible for people to cope with all kinds of stresses. There are many ways of showing appreciation. Here are some examples:

- **Saying 'I appreciate it when . . .'**
- **Telling other people about it**
- **Doing something extra helpful**
- **Giving a small unexpected present**
- **Spending extra time with the person**
- **Arranging something special**

Children are not born knowing how to appreciate and many adults are not too good at it either, so they have to be taught. The easiest way for children to learn is by the example of their parents. But grown ups learn more slowly and may have to be given special lessons in appreciation. Anything subtle is unlikely to have much effect! Once again, good communication is important.

Parent Care

Most parents set out to be the best parents that the world has known or at least better than our own parents. We know only too well what their mistakes were! Soon, however, we discover that being a parent isn't that easy and that it is impossible to get it right all the time.

It doesn't usually take long before parents feel guilty and exhausted. Bringing up children is hard work and the greatest responsibility anyone could have. In order to cope with all this it is vital that parents learn to look after themselves. 'Easier said than done,' you might say, but it is so very important. Parents need for themselves exactly what families need to make life go smoothly – that is:

- **Good communication**
- **Time for the parent**
- **Appreciation**

Good Communication

We all need at least one adult who will listen to us, whom we can trust and with whom we can talk freely. This type of supportive relationship is more important than many people realize. Hopefully a mother and father can talk together in this way, but it isn't always possible. If you find that you can't talk to your spouse in this way it isn't the end of the world, all that is needed is a lot of practice! In the meantime you should find a friend or relative who can support you.

where's mum and dad ?.....

Time for the parent

Parents should arrange to have time for themselves to recover from all the hard work and to enjoy themselves. Mothers and fathers should go out of their way to find some space together without their children present. This isn't as easy as it sounds, so here are some ideas:

- **Insist that children go to bed in good time and that once in bed they do not disturb your time together.**
- **Find a baby sitter that you can trust. If there is no friend or relative able to do this, why not join or start a babysitting circle?**
- **Exchanging children with another family is another way of making a bit of space for yourself. This just means taking it in turns to look after each other's children either during the day or overnight.**
- **Making the arrangements to have some time to yourself or to be together without the children can be difficult. It is best if one parent takes full responsibility for making the arrangements, otherwise nothing may happen.**
- **Don't make excuses. Parents often find all sorts of reasons why they can't have time for themselves. The most common excuse is 'the children need me'. Well, children also need a bit of space for themselves as they grow older. It doesn't do them any good at all to have to hang around their parents all the time or to have parents who have become bogged down at home.**

Appreciation

To be appreciated as a parent is quite unusual. This is sad but true. I think it is because the value and importance of being a parent isn't properly recognized. No medals or awards are given for being a good parent. Of course, if your child happens to be doing well then praise for your child will reflect on you. But most children are not geniuses or stars – they just do averagely well.

One of the best ways of getting appreciation is by giving it. This may seem strange, but it does work. Why not try it out on a friend? If you keep telling them what you appreciate about the way they are bringing up their child, sooner or later they will be telling you about your children and the way you are being a good parent. It isn't cheating to do this. It merely tells the other person that it is OK to give praise and appreciation and that you won't be too embarrassed by it.

Conclusion

Love and affection are obviously the emotions that make a family thrive. Communicating well, having time for each other, and appreciating each family member are all ways of showing your love. It isn't much good having all the right feelings about your family if there isn't enough time for communication and for appreciating each other!

CHAPTER 2

HAPPY FAMILY RELATIONSHIPS

How Close Should Relationships Be?

Relationships are what keep a family together – or blow it apart. It is really important to keep working on family relationships and not take them for granted. It is a bit like being a gardener: plants need to be looked after and protected during bad weather, but just like gardening it is possible to be overprotective and overintrusive in family relationships. People, like plants, need to be kept the right distance from the others – too close and they will smother each other – too distant and they become isolated and vulnerable. A gardener has to keep any weeds and pests away and work hard to provide the best possible environment for growth and development. Caring for a family isn't that much different. Like looking after plants, you have to keep attending to the needs and the relationships of each family member as well as keeping pests away – and it is hard work too!

One of the most difficult things about being a parent is getting the right balance between being too close or being too distant from your child. A parent's wish for a child to be close and dependent and the wish for the child to grow up and become independent, are opposite desires and therefore in conflict with each other.

Every parent has a mental picture of how they would like

their child to be as an adult. A happy, self-confident person who is making the most of life is what most parents would want. But in order to achieve this the child will have to separate away from the close relationships and protective care of their parents. This process of becoming independent involves change and so inevitably something of the past has to be left behind. Seeing your child grow up is therefore likely to provoke a confusing mixture of strong emotions:

● **SADNESS about what has to be left behind**
● **ANXIETY about what will happen**
● **EXCITEMENT about future possibilities**

The relationship between child and parent has to change gradually as the child matures – moving from the close, total protection and security of the parent and child, to a relationship of equals. It takes considerable skill to get the rate of the change just right at each stage of development. For example:

1. *A baby* **must have total protection and intimate care.**
2. *A toddler* **requires close supervision and firm control at all times.**
3. *A young child* **should have carefully planned and supervised experience of coping with the outside world.**
4. *A school-aged* **child needs to learn how to cope alone with the stresses of everyday life in a graduated and safe way.**
5. *Teenagers* **usually make a break for independence whatever you do! Parents need strong nerves to allow their teenager enough freedom while at the same time keeping in check the more extreme desires that young people have to do their own thing.**

IT ISN'T VERY DIFFICULT TO RECOGNISE
OVER-PROTECTIVE PARENTS....

It isn't very difficult to recognize over-protective parents who treat their children as being much younger than their true age. This has the effect of keeping a child immature. But less obviously, many parents treat their children as being older than they actually are. It is all too easy to do this. Children have a powerful urge to grow up and they soon learn how to be very convincing in making demands for more freedom and independence. Here are some of the methods that they use:

- **DEMANDING – the demand is made in such a confident way that parents have agreed to it before they realize that they should have said 'No'.**
- **NAGGING – wearing parents out by going on and on is a favourite technique.**
- **REASONING – children use their own system of**

logic to persuade, such as: 'all the other children do it'. Don't be fooled by this. Try not to join them in their own system of faulty logic!

- **ARGUING** – children often enjoy a good argument, then they can storm off and say how unreasonable you are.
- **TAKING NO NOTICE** – this often works because it is too much hassle to do anything about the child who carries on regardless.
- **BLAMING** – this is a standard technique that children use to make parents feel guilty if they don't go along with everything that the child wants.

It can be easy to go along with any of these persuasive approaches that children use to get their own way and to allow too much freedom and independence too early. A very few children need to be encouraged to be more independent, but most need to be held back for their own safety and have to be very closely supervised until you are sure that you can trust them. Don't let your child persuade you to allow more freedom than you feel confident they can be trusted with.

Parent–Child Relationships

Mothers and Daughters

There is some evidence that as soon as a baby is born the mother will respond differently to a girl than to a boy. Baby girls tend to be held more gently and to have greater skin contact with the mother than boys. Girls are also picked up more quickly than boys when they cry. There is some evidence that boys and girls behave differently right from the start, so it seems probable that the babies themselves influence how their mothers respond to them as well as the other way round.

It is almost inevitable that there will be some competition between two women in one family and it is quite likely that they will compete for the attentions of the father. We often say things like, 'She's daddy's little girl' as a way of recognizing the close bond. Sometimes this rivalry can cause the mother to have feelings of resentment and jealousy, but it is best to accept it as a passing phase.

As a daughter grows older it's quite usual for her to become much closer to her mother and for them to have many interests in common. At this stage it is the father's turn to feel left out! But this close identification with the mother plays an important part in helping a girl to learn about being a woman and the father's role has to change.

During the turmoil of adolescence mothers and daughters often go through a phase of arguing and falling out with each other. Mothers are naturally anxious that their daughters might make the same mistakes as they did at that age – or worse. Negotiating and making compromises between too much freedom and too much restriction is the answer. Fathers can help by acting as a referee, but only if the mother agrees to this.

Some mothers may find their daughters' exploits rather exciting and, wishing to live their own life through their daughter, they become overintrusive (this can also happen between fathers and sons). Without the mother realizing it, the daughter is put under some pressure to do things that her mother always wanted to do when she was younger. All parents do this to some extent and there's not much harm in it as long as it isn't so extreme that the child feels pressurized and restricted in choices she can make.

Fathers and Daughters

The rather special and close relationship that can develop between a father and his young daughter has already been mentioned. There is no harm in it so long as neither the mother nor the other children in the family become jealous. The father must be responsible for making sure that the relationship doesn't become exclusive. In other words, if the daughter will only do things for her father and not for her mother, the relationship may well have become dangerously exclusive.

Fathers tend to play more actively with both sons and daughters than mothers do. This playful relationship can be helpful in defusing tense situations or distracting a child when necessary. A jokey and playful relationship between father and daughter can also avoid the danger of the relationship becoming too emotionally intense. Although the Freudian theory (the Electra complex) about daughters falling in love with their father has little evidence to support it, the father–daughter relationship can quite easily become too close and emotionally charged.

Fathers must always watch out that their relationship with their daughter doesn't become sexualized in any way (and the same can be said for mother–son relationships). Obviously this becomes more of an issue as the daughter grows older. Here are some questions which need to be asked:

- **is she too old to sit on my lap?**
- **should I still help her to wash?**
- **is now the time to stop giving her kisses and cuddles?**
- **should I avoid her seeing me with no clothes on?**

There are no right or wrong answers to these questions. Each will depend on the age of the child, your family's standards of behaviour, and the context in which the situation occurs. It is very difficult for a father to get the right balance in these potentially sexualized situations, so the mother should help to guide the father in what is appropriate and acceptable. Clearly the intimate relationship that is quite natural for a one year old girl to have with her father isn't at all appropriate for a teenage daughter.

Fathers and daughters need to be quite clear about where to draw the line for intimate physical contact. If for any reason the parents can't agree on this, then the daughter must know what her mother thinks is right and feel able to tell the mother if she feels uncomfortable with her father. Sexual abuse within the family only occurs where the rules of relationships are confused and unclear and where there is little understanding of children's needs.

Very strict fathers seem to have a particularly bad effect on their teenage daughters. The evidence suggests that daughters will eventually react against over-restrictiveness and controlling fathers and tend to go out of control and become very disobedient. Sometimes however, daughters of very strict and repressive fathers become withdrawn, distressed, and miserable. The adverse effect of an overstrict father seems to be worse for a girl than it is for a boy.

Fathers and Sons

From the moment of birth of a son there is a potential rivalry between the boy and his father for the attentions of the mother. This competitive relationship may get out of control at any stage, but problems are more likely to occur early on with toddlers or much later when the son is a teenager. The mother is in the best position to keep an eye on this rivalry and to prevent it getting out of hand. Usually just being able to recognize the competitive relationship and to be able to talk about it is enough to improve things.

Most fathers enjoy a rough and tumble with their sons. Unfortunately, these rough games can easily get out of control and end in tears. Often these games take place in the evening, just before going to bed, and so the child becomes over-excited. Once again, the best hope for dealing with this is for the mother to take control and for the parents to agree clear rules for rough and tumble games, such as:

- **no one must get hurt**
- **such games must not happen within an hour of bedtime or mealtimes**
- **they should not go on for more than about 5 minutes**
- **they can be stopped immediately by any family member**

Many fathers want their sons to be outstandingly successful and macho, good at sport, and earning lots of money. This may lead to disappointment if the boy is unambitious, clumsy, or sensitive by nature. The father's expectations can put his son in a very difficult position. If the son manages to be successful and tough this makes him more obviously a competitor with the father: if he doesn't reach his father's expectations, he is seen as a failure – either way, the son can't win. Obviously it is best to be aware of these hidden pressures, and once again it is the mother who is most likely to be able to point this out.

The father–son relationship is usually more authoritarian than that with daughters. This means that fathers are less likely to allow their decisions to be questioned by their sons. Fathers are more likely to use physical force to control a boy's behaviour than they would with their daughters. As a result of this authoritarian relationship there tends to be less trust and frankness between fathers and sons than there is in other family relationships.

One way of resolving the possible tensions in a father–son relationship is for the father to find something that he can enjoy doing with his son. In this way they can become good mates together. A father–son friendship is something worth working hard and long for. The teenage years can cause major problems between a father and son unless enough common ground has been prepared between them in advance.

Often fathers spend very little time with their family. This is partly because they mistakenly believe that to be a good father it is necessary to be successful at work, to earn a lot of money, and to work long hours. This would probably be less of a problem if being a parent had more importance and status attached to it. Until this happens it is necessary to use the father's time at home as effectively as possible. A special time for a father and his son to be together can be helpful (see page 60). This time needs to be specially reserved and protected from any intrusions and interruptions – but it need not be longer than 5–10 minutes.

Mothers and Sons

Although mothers tend to respond to their baby sons in a less intimate way than they do to their daughters, the mother–son relationship is often a very powerful one, especially as the boy grows older. Many mothers see their son as a potential protector and provider.

Sons often find that they get landed with a great deal of responsibility if for any reason their father is absent or unsupportive at home. The son may then be expected to take over some of the father's role and even to act as 'husband substitute' for the mother. There are obvious problems for the boy if this happens and he will tend to become bossy and mature beyond his years.

There is evidence that mothers allow boys more freedom and set them a lower standard of behaviour than for girls. Aggression is more likely to be tolerated in a son than in a daughter. However, when boys grow up they often remember their mothers as being much tougher on them than on their sisters. It may well be that mothers do indeed allow boys to be more aggressive, but eventually clamp down on it in a very tough way when it has gone too far and this is what the sons remember.

Problems can sometimes occur if a mother has had a difficult relationship with her own father or with her son's father. Any characteristic that the boy has that reminds her of this will be likely to get in the way of their relationship and cause the mother to have unjustified bad and rejecting feelings against the child. This problem of relationships can also occur between fathers and daughters where the father has had a difficult relationship with his mother or with the mother of his daughter.

As you can see, parent–child relationships are full of potential problems. But don't worry too much – most of us survive in spite of them! It is only the extreme problems that can cause lasting difficulties. The most important thing is to first recognize that there is a problem so that it can be dealt with early on. Of course all relationships need to be worked at and nurtured all the time. So don't give up!

The Divided Family

Sometimes a family can become divided within the same home: it is as if there are two separate units within the same family. Typical examples might be where a family with two children develops a split – one child becomes close to the father and the other to the mother, or in a single child family, a mother and her child may become so close that the father becomes isolated. This situation usually occurs slowly, so it isn't noticed for a long time. Relationship problems can easily occur in a divided family because the parents and children are set up to oppose each other rather than to work together.

It is quite normal – and indeed very important – to have a clear division in a family, but it should be a horizontal one separating the children from the adults rather than being vertical dividing the parents from each other.

The Normal Family	
Father	Mother
───────────────	
Child	Child

The Split Family	
Father │	Mother
Child │	Child

If you think this problem has occurred in your family it is important to try and reverse the process by changing the alliances and by making a point of doing things as a family and as a parental couple.

Grandparents

Grandparents can enjoy the pleasures of parenthood without the responsibilities; in addition they have much more power and influence on families than might be expected. The combination of power without responsibility may be helpful and constructive but it can also be undermining and even destructive. Grandparents may influence families in several different ways:

● **Your own childhood experiences are very important in determining how you will bring up your own child. Even if you decide that you are certainly not going to be like your own parents, you are still being influenced by them.**

- **Grandparents have strong feelings about their grandchildren and how they should be brought up. They find it difficult, if not impossible, to hold back their opinions. They are experts on childcare and want you to know it!**
- **It is easy to keep the same parent–child relationship going, where you are expected to be obedient and fit in with their wishes as you did when you were a child. Grandparents often forget that their children have grown up and that the relationship is now one of equals.**
- **Grandparents are often indulgent with their grandchildren in a way that can undermine your authority. This needs to be dealt with before it gets out of hand (see below).**
- **In some cases grandparents act as substitute parents if a parent needs extra help and support. This is great, but it does of course increase their influence on both you and your child.**

Because grandparents have so much influence on you and potentially a lot of power over your family, they have to be kept under control even though this is often easier said than done. Grandparents may not like this, but you should remember that you are a fully responsible adult now and your priority must be to your family rather than to your parents. Here are some ideas about how you might manage what can be a very tricky situation.

- **Make it very clear exactly what you expect the grandparents to do with your family and what the family rules of behaviour are.**
- **If the grandparents carry on undermining what you are trying to do in spite of what you have said they should be given a final warning from the parent on their side of the family.**

- **It is best to avoid confrontations with the in-laws. So each parent should deal with their own parents.**
- **If problems continue even after you have given your final warning it is best to restrict the time that the grandparents are able to spend with your family. This limits the undermining that they can do.**
- **Try not to lose contact altogether. It is important for children as they are growing up to know more about their own family background and to learn about the older generation.**

It may seem that I take an unreasonably tough line about grandparents. This is only because their undermining of parents can cause so much damage to family relationships. Fortunately, the majority of grandparents use their power and influence in a positive and supportive way.

Aunts and Uncles

Aunts and uncles seem to play a less important part in family life than they used to. Perhaps this is because family members tend to be more dispersed these days. This is a shame because they can play a very supportive role in family relationships. Their special strength is that they share the same childhood experiences and carry with them the same family traditions. However, this can at times be a source of problems if the old rivalries and bad habits of childhood relationships have continued into adult life.

It is important to leave any rivalries in the past and to try and break old habits that get in the way of being friends. There are several reasons why being on good terms with your child's uncles and aunts is a good idea:

- **They have usually known you for longer than almost anyone else.**

- **Your relationship with them will provide an example of good family relationships for children to copy.**
- **They can give general support for your family.**
- **Cousins can practise friendly relationships with each other while under the close supervision of the family.**
- **Shared family experiences and memories reinforce a sense of belonging together as a family.**

Brothers and Sisters

Arguments and jealousy are the main problems that parents worry about when it comes to the relationship between their children. Jealousy is often the cause of the arguments, but because it is such an important and common problem, it is dealt with separately in Chapter 3.

Apart from dealing with the underlying jealousy, what can parents do to stop arguments between their children? Here are some ideas:

- **Perhaps the most important thing is to establish right from the beginning that squabbling and arguing is just not acceptable in your family. To be successful you will need to keep on taking a very firm line about this and continually teach your children how to be generous and caring to each other.**
- **Avoid arguing with your children. This will only give them practice and they will become even better at arguing with their siblings.**
- **Parents should only argue with each other in private – if at all. Otherwise their children may pick up a few tips on how to say nasty things and how to be really argumentative.**

- **Try to stop an argument as soon as possible, before it has got out of hand. The longer the arguments go on, the more expert the children will become at arguing.**
- **If all else fails, separating the children in different rooms should work. It is a good idea to keep them separated for twice as long as the argument lasted so that there is a clear link between their argumentative behaviour and the separation.**
- **After an argument it helps reinforce your distress and dislike of arguments if you get the children to apologize to each other and to the rest of the family.**

Tensions and arguments tend to happen more frequently in larger families and where space is limited. If the children share the same bedroom, it helps if they can have their own

individual space, even if it is only a shelf or a drawer.

Most children are not naturally kind and considerate, they have to be taught by example and by being told what to do. They also have to be taught how to express their point of view in an acceptable way without getting into an argument. The trouble with arguments is that things get said in the heat of the moment that are regretted afterwards, but the memory of what was said lives on and spoils relationships.

Brothers and sisters are usually very loyal to each other in spite of their disagreements and jealous feelings. It is important that parents realize this and avoid saying things like, 'The children are always arguing. They really hate each other'. This only makes it more difficult for the children to get on together.

You might find it interesting to inquire about how your children get on when you are not there. It is often the case that they get on better, with fewer arguments. It isn't at all unusual for parents to join in their children's arguments and make them even worse!

Conclusion

We have seen that family relationships are both complicated and difficult to keep going smoothly. Is it worth it? Strong relationships are protective and enjoyable. Poor relationships cause more human distress than anything else and tend to be self-perpetuating into the next generation. It would seem that it really is worth continuing to work at improving family relationships. There is a big pay-off for both you and your children.

CHAPTER 3

JEALOUS RELATIONSHIPS

There is nothing very nice about jealousy, but we all experience it. Unfortunately, jealousy is usually a very destructive emotion that can unsettle or even break up a relationship. Jealousy is therefore a sign of danger and it tells you that something needs to be done. Just ignoring jealousy will allow it to grow and feed on itself until it becomes more and more out of control.

Jealousy is a mixed emotion consisting mainly of anxiety and anger, but there is usually some sadness there as well. The anxiety comes from the worry that you might lose something that rightfully belongs to you. The anger is directed at the person who you think has taken it away, and then finally the sadness occurs when you feel that you have lost what you thought was yours. The feelings of jealousy are mostly about relationships rather than about objects.

Envy and jealousy are often confused with each other, but they are not the same at all. Envy is the feeling you have when you want something that rightfully belongs to another person – 'I want his toy, it's better than mine'. On the other hand, jealousy is the feeling that someone else has something that you believe rightfully belongs to you – 'I want his toy, mummy should have given it to me'. In most cases envy involves only two people, but jealousy usually involves three people. This is one of the reasons why jealousy is a much more complicated emotion than envy.

Jealousy is a Normal Emotion

Unfortunately there is no way of escaping from feelings of jealousy, unless you live alone on a desert island! Jealous feelings begin to appear around the age of 2–2½ years. Jealousy then continues to develop over the next 5 or 6 years, by which time your child will hopefully have learnt how to manage and deal with these strong and unpleasant emotions.

The normal jealousy that occurs between children in a family is called **'sibling rivalry'** and it is this rivalry that is the cause of most of the arguments and resentment between brothers and sisters. It may even lead to them falling out with each other so badly that it becomes fixed as a way of life with the result that they may prefer not to keep in touch when they have grown up.

THERE IS NO WAY OF ESCAPING FROM FEELINGS OF JEALOUSLY.....

Although jealousy is a normal emotion, experienced by everyone, there is a lot of variation in how strongly it is felt and how well it is dealt with. This will depend on several different factors:

- **Parents who have not experienced sibling rivalry because they were an only child may have difficulty helping their own children to cope with jealousy and rivalry.**
- **Parents who have experienced a lot of jealousy themselves will probably also find it difficult to deal with their children's jealousy. They are likely to overcompensate and try to avoid their children having any feelings of jealousy, or they may regard jealousy as so natural that nothing needs to be done about it.**
- **A child's personality will influence the strength of the feeling of jealousy. The more 'highly strung' and sensitive the child is, the stronger the feeling will be.**
- **Eldest children are likely to experience more rivalry and jealousy than their brothers or sisters because they are the only ones to have experienced the undivided attention of their parents and they will also have to cope with more new arrivals to the family than any of their siblings.**
- **A very large gap between children may cause stronger feelings of jealousy in the older child because they have experienced a longer time without competition from the younger child. However . . .**
- **A very small age gap can also cause stronger feelings of jealousy because the needs of the children are so similar that there is likely to be more competition between them.**

Expect Jealousy – and prepare for any new arrival to the family

Jealousy is a normal part of any relationship, but particularly so within the family because the relationships are usually that much closer. Everybody in the family can be affected by jealousy: the children, the parents, the grandparents, and even the pets – well, maybe not the goldfish!

Parents can easily become jealous of each other's special relationship with a child. One time when this is particularly likely to occur is around the time of the birth of a baby when fathers easily feel left out of the close mother–child relationship. But later on, it may be the mother who becomes jealous of the father's close relationship – most frequently with a daughter. Don't forget that one parent can

also become jealous of the other's commitment to work or an outside interest.

It certainly shouldn't come as a surprise to find that someone in your family is jealous. In fact you should always be on the look out for feelings of jealousy so that they can be recognized and dealt with before getting out of control.

Unfortunately, feelings of jealousy and rivalry have a tendency to continue and become self-perpetuating. When a child feels jealous, one thing leads to another in the following way:

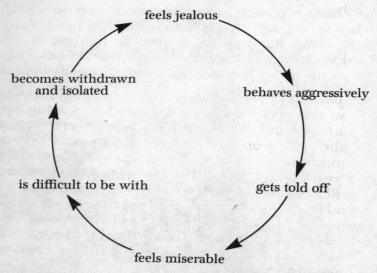

Feelings of jealousy that have been around for a long time may eventually get covered up and hidden away. The jealousy will then come out in unexpected ways, such as hostility, or rejection that seems to be quite unreasonable and excessive. Eventually, unrecognized jealousy may lead to misery and low self esteem.

Any new arrival in the family will inevitably increase feelings of jealousy. It can be expected when a child has a baby brother or sister or if a step-parent/step-sibling joins the family. Less expected is the jealousy that may occur if a friend or relative comes to stay, even if only for a short time.

Emotional and behavioural problems are much less likely to occur if you have been able to prepare your child for a situation where jealousy is predictable, for example the arrival of a new baby to the family. Here are a few guidelines on how you might deal with this situation, but the ideas can easily be modified to cope with any other new arrival to the family:

Preparation for the Arrival of a Baby

Early Preparation

- **If you tell your child about the pregnancy too soon, you will probably get fed up with repeating over and over again when the baby is due to arrive. Your child will probably also get fed up and become uninterested. Children below the age of about 7 or 8 years of age have little concept of time, so they will not see much difference between six months and six weeks. Perhaps the best time to tell a child about a pregnancy is when the baby makes itself known, either by the size of the bulge or by other changes that might cause worry if they have not been explained.**

- **How a child is told is also important. It is a good idea for both parents to be present when the child is told about the baby and if the child is young enough, to sit on the lap of one of the parents. Short and simple explanations are best. Your child will only become confused if you give too much detail or go on for more than a few minutes. Something like this would be OK: 'We are going to have a baby soon. At** the moment it is inside mummy's tummy. Put your hand to her tummy and see if you can feel the baby move. When the baby is born we will all be able to look after it and later on when it gets a bit bigger we will be able to play together with the baby'.

- Try and avoid anyone developing a fixed idea that it is definitely going to be a brother or definitely a sister, unless you have had a scan and know for sure what sex the baby is. In this way you will avoid disappointment all round.
- Your child may go through a stage of asking lots of difficult questions about the baby. You don't have to give long and complicated answers because these only produce even more impossible questions and a great deal of confusion all round. Equally the answers should be truthful. Finding babies under a gooseberry bush is no longer acceptable!
- In your preparations for the new baby, keep a look out for any sign of jealousy developing in your child. It is much easier to deal with if you catch it early.
- Take care not to say too much about the pregnancy and how you are feeling when you are with your child. Children are very quick to pick up worries and fears from their parents.

Late Preparation

- As the expected date of arrival gets closer, it is a good idea to involve the child as much as possible in all the preparations.
- It is best if your child has as little change to the daily routine as possible when the baby is born. If the mother is in hospital it is best if the father or a relative can stay at home to look after the child during this time.

- **Children like to know what is happening, so keep them informed, but keep it simple. You may have to repeat things on several occasions to make sure that they really do know what is going on. Children get some very funny ideas sometimes!**
- **If there is concern about the pregnancy, it is best to tell the child only the minimum so that they can understand why you are worried, but are not made too anxious.**
- **Involving the child in selecting a present that can be given to the baby is a helpful way of channelling any jealousy.**

Introducing the new arrival
- **When your child first meets the new baby, it is better for the baby to be lying in the cot rather than**

being cuddled in your arms. This will make it less likely that your child will feel painfully jealous and also allow you to give more time and attention for your child.

- An exchange of presents between the child and the baby is often helpful in getting the relationship off to a good start. Perhaps the child could give the baby a soft toy and the baby could 'give' a present in return.

- Give your child extra physical contact and extra cuddles.

- Your child can join in with you when you are affectionate to the baby.

- You may find that a special doll could act as a baby substitute to teach your child how to look after the baby and to act as a distraction while you are busy.

I have described the preparations that may be helpful when a new brother or sister comes along. Preparing for any new arrival can be done in much the same way. Most important of all is to be able to predict when jealousy is likely to occur and then to do something about it rather than waiting and hoping that the jealousy will just fade away.

Always Encourage Caring and Responsibility

Children need to be able to recognize when the nasty feelings they have about someone are due to jealousy rather than anything else. In other words – when it is their problem and not the other person's. It is therefore helpful to explain what is happening if you think your child is feeling jealous.

It can be dangerous to neglect a child's feelings of jealousy and it could even be psychologically damaging to do anything to encourage these destructive feelings. Jealousy is such a distressing emotion and it doesn't necessarily fade away with time. In fact if nobody takes any notice it usually gets stronger. On the other hand, if jealousy is suppressed it will probably come out in more sly and hidden ways.

Let the Jealous Child Have Extra Attention

As soon as you notice that your child is feeling jealous and it is getting a bit out of control something needs to be done. One of the best ways of reducing feelings of jealousy and rivalry is to give your child more love and attention. This may seem rather odd because it could look as though you are rewarding aggressive feelings and possibly bad behaviour. However, jealousy causes distress and painful emotions that will produce more and more demanding and aggressive behaviour until something happens to make the jealous person feel better.

Giving your child extra love and attention is a way of showing the child that you understand what it feels like. It is, however, important to get the timing right. If you give the attention every time your child is being aggressive and difficult, it may seem to work at first, but there is a risk that your jealous child will learn that there is more attention to be had by being resentful and badly behaved than for being normal. The best time to give more attention is after the jealous behaviour has stopped, or even better, extra attention should be given in a planned way when you know that you have time and will not be disturbed.

Undivided attention from an adult can have a very positive effect on children, even if it is given for a few minutes only. Perhaps this is because it is quite unusual for a child to be given completely undivided attention. Most parents have other things to do at the same time as being with their children, such as housework or cooking – or just watching the television. So one-to-one, undivided, and exclusive attention is rare and special. This special time is sometimes called 'High Quality Time' or 'Golden Time'. Here are some ideas about how to organize this time with your child:

- High quality time is usually much more effective if it is one-to-one.
- Carefully plan a time when you know you will be free for a while.
- Make sure that you won't be disturbed during the special time.
- It may help to go into a separate room where there are no distractions.
- Let your child know that this is their very own special time.
- Find something that you both enjoy doing and that requires you to face each other and talk to each other for most if not all the time.
- Watching the TV together isn't much use – you can do this just as well separately and you won't be able to pay attention to each other.
- Playing a card or board game is easy enough and talking with each other or making something together is even better.
- Occasionally it may help to do something really special together, such as going out for the day somewhere interesting.
- Five to ten minutes is usually long enough. Your child will become bored and irritable if the time is too long – you may become fed up as well. It's best to stop when both of you would like to carry on for a bit longer.
- If you are not enjoying your time together, the chances are that your child isn't either so it won't do much good. Try again another time.

- **If other people in the family become jealous that they are not getting the same attention, remind them that they don't need as much at the present time, or if they do, that their time for special attention will come.**

Giving special time to a child in this way is one of the most 'therapeutic' and helpful things that parents can do when their child is distressed. Just giving this High Quality Time for ten minutes a day for a few days may be all that is needed to get things back to normal. Not surprisingly, adults can also benefit from giving each other High Quality Time!

Often Jealous Children Show Some Babyish Behaviour – Which Should Pass

Stress of any kind will tend to make a child behave like a much younger child. This is called regression and it involves the child going backwards to an earlier stage of development. Jealous feelings are certainly stressful and so it is not surprising that it causes regression in children – and of course in adults also. The amount of regression depends on:

- **How bad the stress is – the worse the stress the greater the regression.**
- **The stage of development that the child has reached – regression in older or more mature children is often less obvious than in young children.**
- **The personality of the child – children who are sensitive and vulnerable will regress further than children who have a tough and easy-going personality.**

Regression can cause a whole range of babyish behaviour and on the whole skills that have recently been gained are the ones that go first. For example, a child who has recently become dry may start wetting again: a child who has just started to talk may stop talking. Some of the most common regressive behaviours are shown in the list below:

- **Tempers**
- **Babyish talk**
- **Babyish play**
- **Clinging**
- **Demanding**
- **Moodiness**
- **Irritability**
- **Wetting**
- **Soiling**

Of course all these behaviours can occur quite normally, but if they are due to regression then they will come as a definite change from the way the child normally behaves and the distress that caused the regression should be fairly obvious. Also the immature behaviour can be expected to occur at much the same time as the stress.

It is important to recognize and understand regressive behaviour because it occurs as a normal and expected reaction to stress. It isn't just a case of the child being difficult and bloody minded. Some degree of regression as a result of stress is almost if not totally impossible to avoid and this is just as true for adults as well.

This regressed, babyish behaviour should gradually fade away and be replaced by more normal mature behaviour within 4–6 weeks of the stressful event. If the immature behaviour persists, there is probably something that is keeping it going, such as:

- **The child is still under stress.**

- The behaviour has become a habit and is now self-perpetuating, just like nail biting or thumb sucking. In other words it has become automatic and occurs without the child really thinking about it.
- Your child has discovered that regressive behaviour is a good way of getting attention – so it is worthwhile carrying on.
- Perhaps you have become used to responding to your child's immature behaviour and it has become a habit for you to treat the child as much younger.

Usually Jealousy Gets Worse If You Treat Children Identically

It is obvious for all to see how painful and destructive jealousy can be. So it isn't surprising that parents try to make things better by being fair and equal in the way they treat their children. Some parents go to great lengths to be fair and to give their children exactly the same in attention, presents, food, and clothes. Unfortunately treating children identically only makes jealousy worse, for the following reasons:

- It is inappropriate to treat children of different sexes and different ages in the same way. As children grow older their needs become increasingly different and they will soon let you know that they think you are being unfair.
- It is *impossible* to be equal and identical in your treatment of the children. If you buy toys of the same value the chances are that one or other child will be dissatisfied and jealous of the other. Even if you give them exactly the same toy, the children are likely to look for any tiny difference to be jealous about.

SOME PARENTS GO TO **GREAT LENGTHS** TO TREAT CHILDREN **IDENTICALLY**....

- **The more you treat children in the same way the more they will look for differences. Meal times are a good example of this: if you try and serve out equal portions of food all the time, you will soon find that they are measuring each bit of food and counting every pea to make sure that they are not missing out.**
- **If children are protected from jealous feelings when they are young they won't learn how to deal with jealousy and will find it difficult to cope with as they grow older.**

Children have to learn that life can be unfair and that people are not always treated equally. From the very beginning children are born unequal, but that does not mean that some are better or more special than others. It is more important to work hard to help children feel that they are special and unique in themselves. They will then be less bothered by feelings of jealousy and rivalry. If children feel confident that their individual needs are understood by their parents, they will accept being treated differently and will not be so jealous.

In this way children will learn to accept the 'give and take' of everyday life. Sometimes you get what you want – and sometimes you don't. In fact children are usually very good at understanding that for a while their brother or sister may need more attention than they do – provided that the reason for this is briefly explained to them and that they know that they will have attention when they need it.

Sharing and Caring, Unlike Jealousy, Has to be Taught

Children learn how to care for and look after others by watching their parents and by their own experience of how they are treated. But as well as learning by example, most children have to be taught how to share and care. A few children are very good at looking after people, but others have to be told over and over again until they have got the message. Obviously the earlier you start this teaching, the better.

Parents are often surprised at how selfish children can be, but this is quite normal for young children. It is a good idea to get in first and teach your child how to share, rather than to wait for them to be selfish and then tell them that it is wrong. As your child grows older you should carry on teaching them about sharing until you are sure that your child will behave in this way automatically. It may take years and years, so don't give up!

Conclusion

Jealousy is a normal emotion that everyone experiences at one time or another. It is important to recognize jealousy as soon as possible and to nip it in the bud before it gets out of hand. Although jealousy can be so damaging and destructive, there are many constructive things that you can do to avoid problems. I wonder if you noticed that the subheadings in this chapter are based on the word JEALOUS?

J. – Jealousy is a normal emotion

E. – Expect jealousy — and prepare for any new arrival to the family

A. – Always encourage caring and responsibility

L. – Let the jealous child have extra attention

O. – Often jealous children show some babyish behaviour – which should pass

U. – Usually jealousy gets worse if you treat children identically

S. – Sharing and caring, unlike jealousy, has to be taught

CHAPTER 4
MAKING FRIENDS

Developing Friendships

It takes some time to teach a child how to cope with social relationships. Even as adults, most of us are still learning about relationships and trying to get them right. Children

have to have developed some idea of themselves as a separate individual before they can have much idea about friendships. This stage is reached at about two and a half years old when children start using 'I' when they talk about themselves.

Relationships at the toddler stage are very basic because they are only just beginning to recognize others as being separate from themselves and they still have no real concept of time and permanence. At this age friends come and go rather easily and they don't have the same emotional significance as they can do when children are older.

Friendships become much more important as children develop a clearer idea about what sort of person they are. A self concept is developed around 7–8 years old and after this stage has been reached children will tend to pick friends who fit in with how they see themselves or how they would like to be. For example:

- **Bright children will mix with other bright children.**
- **Sporty children will naturally join together.**
- **An unpopular child may try to be friendly with the popular children.**
- **The bright child who feels a failure may seek out other failures.**
- **The child with a poor self image will usually join up with other children who behave badly.**

You can see that children tend to choose friends who are either very similar to themselves or who seem to be quite different. If a child chooses a friend who is obviously different from them it may well be that this is because they want to be like them or they feel they *are* like them.

It sounds a bit complicated? Well it's even more so since we have only considered one half of the friendship. The friend will also have their own reasons for being part of the relationship. This is one of the reasons why friendships often don't work out: each partner is looking for something different from the relationship.

Learning about Friendships

Learning about friendships is a complicated two-way process. It involves learning about yourself as well as your friend. One of the main ways that children learn what sort of person they are is by how other people relate to them. Parents have the most influence early on, but as children grow older friends can also play a big part.

If other children keep saying, 'we don't like you' and are going out of their way to avoid a child, that child will soon begin to feel that he or she isn't nice to know. So children who have problems forming relationships may come to see themselves as bad and unlikeable. Children who have developed a poor self image may well seek out other children who feel or behave the same way as they do.

As children learn about friendships they need to have some supervision so that the learning process isn't too painful. When children are young they need to practise with others in a safe way where the making and breaking of relationships isn't taken too seriously. This normally happens at play school and later on at school.

Parents can help by making sure that these early relationships don't become too serious. Seeing your child's relationships in adult terms is an easy mistake to make. It isn't unusual for us to say to a young child, 'I see you have a boy/girl friend' in a way that implies it is like an adult relationship. Although this is meant as a joke, the child usually doesn't appreciate it.

Many children find relationships difficult. The development of friendships is a very subtle process and each person has their own unique way of managing it. It takes time to learn how to make friends and which person to choose as a friend. Here are some guidelines:

- **Children vary a lot in how easily they form friendships.**
- **Most children need more help and guidance with their friendships than you might expect.**
- **It is worth remembering that children tend to copy their parents in the way they form relationships.**
- **In the early stages of learning about friendships (up to about 8 years old) your child will require a high level of supervision when with friends, to ensure that all goes well.**
- **As children grow older the supervision can be more distant, for example by being in another room or by checking what they are doing from time to time.**
- **Many children have difficulty in forming relationships and this is not necessarily a sign of disturbance in the child. Some perfectly normal children prefer to be on their own.**

Supervising Relationships

Young children need help and supervision when they are learning about friendships. As a rough guide you can expect some form of relationship difficulty to occur within five minutes for 5 years olds and younger. By 8 years old children should be able to play together reasonably well for fifteen minutes and at secondary school age most children can manage an hour unsupervised together.

One way of helping your child to develop and learn about relationships is to invite selected children to come to your home so that you can supervise them carefully. Here are some suggestions about how you could organize this:

- When you start inviting children to come and play, only have one at a time.
- Only invite children who you think will get on well with your child.
- Don't feel bad about being selective over which friend you invite to your home.
- If you feel a particular friend is a bad influence on your child, it is quite reasonable to tell your child to keep away from them.
- When you invite a child to your home, it is a good idea to keep the visit short and happy. The longer they stay, the more likely it is that there will be tears or arguments. As soon as the children can cope with a short time together, you can gradually increase the length of the visit.
- If the parent of the friend comes too, remember to

and then **she** said.... she **did** and do you know.... she *didn't!*... good **heavens!!**

REMEMBER TO **CONTINUE TO SUPERVISE**.....

continue to supervise and don't get distracted by interesting adult talk.

- **A common problem occurs when the friend's parent has different standards of discipline and behaviour from yours. Many friendships have come to grief in this way. It is therefore a good idea to sort out with the other parent who is in charge of what. A reasonable plan is to agree that you make the rules in your house and they in theirs. Whatever you agree, don't forget to tell the children!**

It isn't easy for children to be able to distinguish between good and bad friends. Learning by making mistakes isn't unreasonable, but children do need to be protected from their worst mistakes. Parents recognize how delicate friendships can be and often delay too long before intervening in their children's relationship difficulties. This is particularly the case if they have chosen a friend who is leading them astray.

You may need to be very firm about stopping your child from mixing with children who are causing problems. This isn't difficult with young children but as they grow into adolescence it becomes more difficult. Nevertheless this shouldn't stop you from expressing a clear view on the matter. If you are sure that the friendship is having a bad effect on your child there are several things that you can do:

- **Gradually guide your child away from the bad friendship.**
- **Insist that your child has no further contact with them.**
- **Invite friends home who you think are OK.**
- **Keep your child busy with other activities.**
- **If all else fails you could move house or change schools.**

It is obviously a bit extreme to have to move house in order to avoid children who you think are having a bad influence on your child. However, children can have a major effect on each other and sometimes a group of children get together and form anti-social gangs. If other parents in your area don't want to do anything about it you may find that there is little that you can do on your own, especially if your own child is easily led.

Shyness

The first sign of shyness is seen in very young children who from the age of about 6 months onwards show 'stranger anxiety' (see my book *Worries and Fears*). For most children this is a passing phase, but for some the anxiety continues and is often associated with separation anxiety as well. A typically shy child will behave quite normally within the family, but will be clingy and anxious in any unfamiliar situation. This can cause problems when the child has to go to school and do things independently of the family.

From about 8 years onwards children become much more aware of themselves in relation to others and start to develop social anxieties. At this stage children begin to worry about things like:

- **what will they think of me?**
- **am I doing the right thing?**
- **does she like me?**
- **they probably think I am a fool**

These worries are shared by most of us, but some children feel them to a painful extent. Hence the expression 'painfully shy'. However, even the most shy and unassured child can be helped to be more confident socially. The important thing with shy children is to plan social contacts carefully in advance and to take things very slowly with only gradual steps towards closer relationships.

Shyness is usually associated with a lack of self-confidence, although shy children may be quite confident at home and in situations that don't involve social relationships. One way of helping children to overcome shyness is to boost their self-confidence.

Self-confidence can't be developed on praise alone. It is success and achievement that build up confidence and this can only happen if your child has actually done something. In other words, confidence comes from action and activity – from 'having a go' rather than avoiding situations and being passive.

Some children seem to be naturally confident and sail through life's problems with very little worry. Other children are natural worriers and are often shy as well. They quickly lose confidence and become anxious when difficulties arise. Although some of this may be due to a lifelong personality characteristic, much of it is due to life experiences and it is this part that you can have some influence over. It is important to recognize lack of confidence in your child at an early stage, because it can become a fixed way of life if it is ignored. The following signs may indicate that a child lacks self-confidence.

- **avoiding doing things that might be difficult**
- **hesitating before doing even slightly difficult tasks**
- **frequently asking for reassurance**
- **expecting failure**
- **often asking for help**
- **thinking in a negative way and being pessimistic**
- **being quiet and withdrawn**
- **repeatedly asking questions where the answer is obvious**
- **acting big and being over-confident**

The special risk for children with low self-confidence is that they will avoid activities. They will therefore have little chance of making things better and get stuck in a vicious circle. Children who continue to lack confidence in themselves are likely to find it difficult to form relationships and will often be shy with strangers. Fortunately there are many things that you can do to help, such as:

- Give extra praise for everyday activities especially if the job has been done well or without being asked. Even something like cleaning the teeth, laying the table, or putting toys away properly deserves a comment.
- Set up situations where you know that your child will be able to succeed. Start with something that you know can be achieved quite easily and very gradually make the task harder, but never before the previous stage has been successfully achieved.
- Protect your child from failure.
- Avoid using negative statements about your child, such as: 'you are hopeless', 'I have no confidence in you', 'I knew you wouldn't be able to do it'.
- Make sure that you haven't set standards for your child that are too high.
- Show that you do have confidence in your child – and say so too.
- Point out and emphasize every success.
- Tell your friends, in front of your child, how pleased you are with any achievement.
- Deal with any jealousy that your child may have, because this emotion is closely linked with a lack of confidence.
- Make sure that no one is undermining what you are doing, especially other relatives or people at school.

● **Consistent loving care and clear discipline will protect your child's self-confidence and lead to a feeling of security.**

You may think to yourself 'well there is nothing new there – I'm doing it all the time'. Most parents think that they give a lot of praise, and this may be true for the first few years, but not many parents keep it going right the way through childhood. Think of the amount of praise and attention that toddlers have when they first start to walk. Every small step is applauded. Children who are shy and lack self-confidence need this kind of powerful praise if they are to change.

Special Relationships

The Crush

As children grow older and develop moral values (age 8 years and onwards), they tend to see things as either very good or very bad. At this stage children often have heroes and heroines and for some children this can become an extremely powerful emotional relationship. Hero worship is well recognized in children and teenagers, but it can also occur in adults. The hero or heroine becomes invested with every admirable quality imaginable to the point of unreality.

An emotional 'crush' on somebody is usually a passing phase that requires watching but no further action. However, if the idolized person is somebody who is seen every day, rather than a pop star or sporting celebrity, the relationships can get out of hand and become too intense. It is difficult to be sure just when a 'crush' relationship is getting out of control, but one of the best indications is when the relationship starts to exclude other people or becomes embarrassing. Here are some ideas about how you might deal with a child with a crush.

- **Deal with the crush as delicately as possible.**
- **Banning the relationship causes distress and strengthens the emotional aspect of the relationship.**
- **General, open discussion about relationships should help.**
- **There is no harm in letting the child know that you disapprove of relationships that exclude others.**
- **Encourage other relationships.**
- **Involve yourself in the relationship so that it is less exclusive.**

The Enemy

In just the same way that children have crushes so they may also develop a strong feeling of hate towards somebody. These destructive emotions are often based on fear and prejudice. Sometimes the hated enemy is somebody who is seen as a threat, but at other times the hate seems quite illogical. In this case the hate may well be sparked off by a characteristic that the person dislikes about themselves.

Strong irrational dislikes of other people can easily be picked up from others and it isn't unusual to find that parents and their children share the same pet hates about people. Because children tend to follow the example of their parents in identifying the hated enemy, it is largely up to parents to make sure that their children do not become over-prejudiced about people. Equally it is important that children do learn to discriminate between those who have a good influence and those who are potentially dangerous.

The Victim

Some relationships are based on one person dominating the other. There may be nothing wrong with this – indeed some people enjoy being dominated. However, any relationship that involves intimidation is likely to be damaging and destructive and the repeated use of deliberate aggression by a powerful person against a victim is unacceptable.

Some children seem to become victims very easily and they appear to set themselves up to be picked on. A typical victim has the following characteristics.

- **sensitive and quiet**
- **reacts to aggression with tears and withdrawal**
- **lacks confidence**
- **lonely and isolated**
- **unaggressive and unlikely to retaliate**
- **appears vulnerable and weak**

These qualities are probably lifelong and part of the child's personality. The normal response from parents is to protect any child who is a victim, but this doesn't really help in the long run. Children who get picked on regularly need special training to teach them how to deal with people who want to intimidate them. Here are some ways of helping a child victim:

- **Do everything you can to boost their self-confidence (see pages 75-6).**
- **Teach the victim to become more assertive in the way they express their wishes. For example, learning to speak more loudly may help. Shouting, 'Go away' can be very effective.**
- **The victim should be helped to avoid giving signals that say, 'I am a victim'. They should stand tall and**

learn to look their aggressor straight in the eyes.
- **Learning some form of self-defence such as judo or karate may help to build up confidence.**

Of course teaching victims to defend themselves in this way is expecting them to do something that is most unnatural for them. A lot of practice will be needed in a safe place and until they are competent at self protection, they should have a 'minder' to look after them.

The Bully

Unfortunately some children are much more aggressive than others. They will tend to seek out victims to dominate. The bully usually comes from a home where there are few restrictions on aggressive behaviour. The typical bully has the following characteristics:

- **impulsive and aggressive in all situations**
- **dominant and strong**
- **enjoys violence**
- **little feeling for the victim**
- **good self esteem**

The problem with bullies is that they tend to continue to have relationships based on their aggressive domination of another person. This really is a vicious circle. Aggressive children tend to provoke their parents to use coercive physical power to control them. This in turn encourages the child to use violence in relationships. Fortunately there are things that can be done to prevent this aggressive behaviour:

- **Start early on before it is too late. Aggression in children over the age of 8 years has a strong tendency to continue.**

- **Teach the child to be aware of others' needs and feelings.**
- **Avoid any exposure to violence at home or on the TV/video/cinema.**
- **Keep the aggressive child under close supervision to prevent violent behaviour.**
- **Training in aggression control can be helpful. This needn't be anything too complicated. Work out the siutations that provoke aggression and look at alternative ways of dealing with them. A lot of practice will be needed!**

The Loner

Most children go through phases when they want to be alone, and in most cases parents worry about it more than they need to. Children take many years to learn about friendships and it is natural to prefer to play alone if the alternative usually ends up in an argument or ruined game. Up to 7–8 years of age children rarely form firm friendships and after that many children still prefer to keep other children at a distance. Here are some guidelines for coping with the loner:

- **If the child seems happy as a loner, there is no need to worry too much.**
- **If your lonely child would like to have friends but can't manage it, ask your child what kind of help he/she would like (see page 70, supervising relationships).**
- **Boost confidence in relationships by practising with easy ones first – for example relationships within the family or with younger children.**
- **If nothing seems to work, it is best to accept that your child is made to be a loner and will only change if it is really necessary to do so.**

IT IS BEST TO ACCEPT THAT YOUR CHILD IS MADE TO BE A **LONER**.....

Conclusion

The art of developing a friendship is something that has to be learned. It is a delicate process that requires a high level of supervision in its early stages and a lot of practice before children get it right. Most relationship problems such as shyness and loneliness can be resolved and need not carry on into adult life, but aggressive relationships can become self-perpetuating unless actively prevented at an early stage.

CHAPTER 5

ALTERNATIVE FAMILIES

Many of you reading this chapter will be, or have been, single parents. Some of you will have experienced the divorce of your own parents when you were a child and you may also have experienced some form of substitute parenting. You will know better than anyone else about the problems and pain of broken relationships. Those of you who haven't been through this experience are likely to be shocked by how often parental relationships break down and how serious the consequences are for the children.

I am afraid that the facts are grim and the failure of family relationships often causes deep emotional wounds. However, there are things that can be done to prevent the wounds in the first place (outlined in Chapters 1–3). There are also things that can be done to reduce the severity of the wound or to promote healing so that the scar that remains isn't so obvious or handicapping.

If you have first-hand knowledge of these problems, please try not to feel too guilty or angry. What has happened has happened and it is best left in the past. Guilt and anger make us do all the wrong things – such as being overindulgent or blaming other people. I hope that reading this chapter will help you to have a better understanding of children who have experienced family breakdown and know more about what can be done to help them.

Parenting Alone

The divorce rate has more than doubled over the past 20 years to the point where about one in three marriages breaks down. Fortunately not all these broken marriages involve children, but it is estimated that about 1 in 5 children will receive alternative care outside the standard two parent family at some time during their childhood.

One in seven families will have only one parent for a period, and this is mostly due to marital breakdown, although about 20 per cent of one parent families have never been married and 10 per cent of one parent families are caused by the death of a parent. About 1,600,000 children are being brought up in a one parent family in Great Britain. Although living in a one parent family is quite common, more than half of the lone parents have either remarried or are cohabiting within three years of the family breakdown.

Parenting alone may come about through choice, through separation or divorce, or as a result of the death of a parent. But whatever the cause, the one parent family is seriously disadvantaged in many different ways:

- **Average income is 40 per cent of that of two parent families.**
- **More than 50 per cent of one parent families are living in poverty.**
- **More than 1,000,000 children in one parent families are being brought up on Supplementary Benefit.**
- **About half of lone mothers work either part-time or full-time.**
- **Sixty per cent of one parent families are dependent on the local authority for housing (compared with 20 per cent of two parent families).**
- **Most one parent families live in deprived inner city areas.**

Many single parents are highly successful in bringing up their children and are very resourceful in finding ways of coping with these disadvantages. Later on in this chapter I shall outline some of the ways of protecting children from the effects of these life stresses over which they have so little control.

Separation and Divorce

At any one time about 40 per cent of one parent families are headed by a divorced mother and 20 per cent have a separated mother. About 10 per cent of one parent families (usually with older children) are headed by a father. Of course there isn't that much difference between these families. They have all experienced the breakdown of previously loving relationships and have lost the care of one of the parents.

Although divorce may result in an improvement of the life of many of the adults involved, only a minority of children can be said to benefit. In many cases it is a disaster that causes a tidal wave of problems that continues for years, if not for a lifetime.

One in five children (two in five in America) can be expected to experience the separation of their parents before they are 16 years old. The majority of these parents will remarry and almost half of these remarriages will eventually fail. The massive increase in divorce and the resulting high rate of disturbance in children would be called an epidemic if it were due to an illness.

Divorce doesn't occur as a single traumatic event but rather it is part of a process of failed and sour relationships that may have started to go wrong many years previously and which will often continue to be painfully distressing for years after the divorce. In a minority of cases both parents feel relieved that the relationship is over and done with. But there is really no such thing as a happy divorce as far as children are concerned.

It is the repeated experience of unhappy and aggressive relationships over a long period that seems to be particularly damaging to children. Here are some of the experiences that many of the children of broken families have to cope with *after* a divorce or separation:

- **Experiencing the continuing anger and resentment between their parents**
- **Having a severe and lasting drop in their standard of living**
- **Feeling rejected and unwanted, anxious and miserable**
- **Coping with a parental remarriage or cohabitation**
- **Facing the difficulties of forming new step-relationships**
- **Dealing with the problems and emotions of access**
- **Watching their parents experience great distress**

There is very little difference as far as the child is concerned between divorce and separation. The impact is much the same. An official divorce *may* help a child to realize that the separation is permanent and disputes between the parents have been settled by the court. Unfortunately, however, most children continue to hope and fantasize that their parents will get together again, and it isn't unusual for parental disputes to continue in spite of court rulings.

Most children will eventually agree that their parents are better off living apart. At the same time most children express a deep feeling of sadness and distress that their parents are not together. And it isn't unusual for children to find that there are more stresses to cope with after the divorce than before. Most children eventually lose regular contact with the separated parent and generally receive remarkably little support from them.

The Short Term Effects of Divorce

It is the disturbed relationships and distressed emotions of separation and divorce that cause problems for children, more than the actual loss of a parent. The death of a parent also causes emotional disturbance, but it is less extensive and there are fewer adverse effects on future relationships than after divorce.

The effects of divorce are therefore due to events before, during, and after the actual separation itself. The most common effects of divorce on children are outlined below:

Younger Children
- tempers and aggression
- babyish, demanding behaviour
- soiling and wetting
- bewilderment
- anxiety and clinging behaviour
- self blame for the divorce
- boys are more affected than girls

Older Children
- underachieving at school
- low self esteem in girls
- behaviour problems at home and/or school
- depression
- conflicts of loyalty
- yearning for the absent parent
- anger at custodial parent
- fantasies of reconciliation
- girls and boys are equally affected

It has been estimated that about 80 per cent of children become significantly disturbed in the year after their parent's divorce. Most of these children will be able to function fairly normally in the following year, but about 20 per cent remain disturbed enough for them to have difficulty coping with everyday life.

The Long Term Effects of Divorce

The long term effects of any traumatic event are always difficult to assess; however, there is now evidence from several long term (5–10 year) follow up studies of children who have experienced the divorce of their parents which show the most frequent long term effects to be:

- **anxiety and separation problems**
- **boys and girls more aggressive than usual**
- **anti-social problems in boys and girls**
- **psychiatric problems**
- **academic difficulties for boys**
- **sexual relationship problems for girls**

All these problems occur significantly more frequently than in non-separated families living together in intact homes. More than half the parents have found a new partner within 3 years, but parental remarriage seems to present particular problems for girls. This is just one example of the different ways divorce affects boys and girls.

Another frequent finding is that boys who are brought up in the absence of a father have been noted to have a higher rate of academic difficulties than expected. On the whole, it appears that younger boys and older girls are more vulnerable to the stresses of divorce. As adults, both men and women who have experienced the divorce of their parents are more likely to divorce themselves.

Surviving Divorce

Although many children suffer long term consequences

following the divorce or separation of their parents, some children seem to adjust to it better than others. There is some evidence that where the divorce has taken place before a child can retain a memory of the event (before 3 years old), the long term effect of divorce results in less aggression and less general disturbance than usual. Here are some of the ways in which children can be protected from divorce damage and be helped to cope better with marital breakdown:

- **continuity of care and effective parenting**
- **maintaining contact with the absent parent**
- **parents being able to meet their own emotional needs**
- **having as few life changes as possible**
- **having a good self esteem**
- **being able to make adjustments before the divorce**
- **agreement on child care between the parents**
- **avoiding prolonged divorce disputes**

The acute effects of the divorce should be largely resolved within a year. So, if there are continuing problems with children after this time or if the level of distress is really very high you should think of the following possibilities:

- **The arrival of a step-parent has caused renewed distress and confusion.**
- **The remaining parent is still distressed. Children are usually much more aware of their parent's distress than we realize. This is particularly true in the case of younger children.**
- **Unsatisfactory access to the separated parent is a very common cause of continuing distress.**
- **There is still some work to be done to establish the new family relationships.**
- **The unsettled behaviour which occurred as a result**

of the change in family relationships has now become a habit and is self-perpetuating. If this is the case, you will have to be very firm in dealing with the bad behaviour and very sympathetic in dealing with the upset emotions – a difficult balance.

● Parents often feel very guilty about the distress they have caused their children. This guilt usually results in overindulgence which only encourages bad behaviour and stores up problems for later on.

Custody and Access

Custody and access arrangements can also help or hinder adjustment. There has been a fashion for joint custody and for shared care between the parents. There is some evidence that supports these options as better than others, but it is only parents who have reasonably good relationships who are going to agree to this type of arrangement. What seems to be absolutely critical is that the children should know to whom they belong and who makes the final decisions about their future.

The arrangements that are made for access to the non-custodial or non-residential parent can make all the difference to how children cope after a divorce. There are several factors to keep in mind when arranging access for children:

● *Predictability* is more important than *frequency* of access.
● *Enjoyment* of the access visit is more important than its *duration*.
● Children who are older than about 8 years can express a reasonably independent view about what access they would like and this should be taken into account when making arrangements.

● **Teenagers should be able to make their own arrangements for access.**

One of the main reasons for having access is to maintain contact with the absent parent. After the separation there is a new arrangement of the family – so the parent who leaves also has to expect a new relationship with the children. The relationship becomes more like that of an uncle or aunt rather than that of a parent. This may sound a bit extreme, but there is no way anyone can carry out parental responsibilities effectively by remote control.

Access arrangements that share the responsibility and time spent with each parent may seem very reasonable. But unfortunately this divided care arrangement is very likely to lead to confusion and problems sooner or later. Where a child spends the week with one parent and the weekend with the other, this is very similar to split care. Although the weekend is only 2 days against the 5 during the week, the weekend is a time for the family and for relaxing and having fun together. It is therefore just as significant as all the weekdays put together. Divided care – sometimes called 'shared care' has many potential problems:

● **It is easy for the child to play one parent off against the other.**
● **It is easy for one parent to blame the other for any problems.**
● **If you have to tell your child off just before the change over, there is no time for either of you to make things right again.**
● **Some children find it difficult to adjust to living in two separate families.**
● **It is easy for a parent or a child to threaten that the child will go and live with the other parent. This can cause feelings of insecurity.**
● **It is difficult to get on the same wavelength as the**

children and to know what they are really thinking and feeling.

● **Children in divided care often feel like yo-yos going between the parents.**

It is generally better for the children of divorce to be quite clear where they belong and to have a definite base from which they visit their other parent. The custodial parent should normally have full care and control of the children and have the final say in any decisions that affect the children. It isn't reasonable to have full parental rights without taking on the full parental role for day-to-day childcare.

Step-Parents

The 'wicked step-parent' is mostly a myth and the

but you're too **PRETTY** and **NICE** to be a **PROPER** stepmother!!...

and why haven't you locked us **IN THE SHED** or given us **DRY BREAD** for supper?...

problems that occur with step-parents are mainly due to underestimating the high level of stress that children and their parents experience when a relationship is ended. Here are some of the common causes of problems in step relationships:

- **The loss of a parent is distressing to any child. In the period before the loss, both parents will be under stress and will therefore have less time and energy to give to the child. The separation or death will leave the remaining parent with many practical and emotional problems which inevitably means that it is difficult to meet all the child's needs.**
- **The process of the parent and step-parent making a new relationship can be expected to take attention away from the child and to cause jealousy.**
- **So, the child loses out before, during and after the loss of the natural parent. This naturally makes the child angry and resentful. Gaining a step-parent is rarely seen by the child as a great blessing.**
- **Step-parents bring with them many different ideas on discipline and childcare, which often causes inconsistency and resentment.**
- **If a step-parent brings their own children with them to join the family, jealousy between the children is often very strong, particularly if they are close in age.**

Being a step-parent is full of problems, but a lot can be done to improve things if the parent and step-parent sit down and carefully work out an agreed plan for how they are going to deal with children's anger, distress, and confusion. Here are some ideas:

- **Following the loss of a parent for whatever reason, children experience extremely strong feelings of**

anger, resentment, misery, and worry. It is important to realize that these feelings are at the root of
much of the children's difficult and disturbed
behaviour.

- The new parental partners need to agree on how
they are going to discipline the children. A consistent, firm, and fair approach and a united front
is very important to help the children to feel more
secure.

- As with all children who are distressed, it helps to
spend extra time with them and to give extra attention. But being soft and indulgent usually makes
things worse.

- It is best if the step-parent takes on a parental role
as far as possible, especially with younger children. This is a very sensitive issue. The fact is that
the step-parent is living at home as a substitute
parent. If this reality isn't recognized then it is
likely that a split will occur within the family as
described on (page 44).

The development of a good relationship between a step-
parent and step-child takes time and effort and patience.
The most important thing for step-parents to remember is
that the anger and aggression that is often directed at them
is really meant for the natural parents. Don't take it too
personally!

Adoption and Fostering

Children who are adopted or fostered will have experienced a separation from *both* parents, rather than just one.
Adoption and fostering are similar in many ways, although
the commitment of adoption may make a child feel more
secure. This is one of the reasons why the outcome of

adoption is generally rather better than for fostered children. Both these groups of children do better than most children of single parents – mostly because these substitute parents are specially chosen for their ability to parent well and they don't have the same social adversities to cope with. These are general findings and may not apply in any individual case – there are always exceptions to the rule. Much will depend on the reason why alternative parents were necessary.

Very young children who have been adopted or fostered before they are 3 years old will have little or no memory of living anywhere else and they will become strongly attached to their substitute parents. This emotional attachment continues even though they realize later that their parents are elsewhere. The younger a child is brought into substitute parenting therefore, the better the outcome is likely to be. However, some children who have come into foster care or adoption when they are quite old can do surprisingly well. A lot will depend on the following factors:

- **the reason why the child has to leave the parents**
- **the child's past experience before being adopted or fostered**
- **the child's personality**
- **the presence or absence of emotional or behavioural problems**
- **the capability of the substitute parents**
- **the type of contact with natural parents**

Both adopted and fostered children tend to become more unsettled during their adolescence. If they do present significant problems they are likely to go right over the top and a very strong nerve will be needed. The big issue will always be, 'why didn't my parents want me?' Adopted and fostered children will need to be continually reminded of how much they are wanted and loved in their present home.

Another issue for older children in substitute care is, 'where are my parents now?'. They may becme quite preoccupied with this question, but often don't actually want to be put in touch with them. In this situation it is often best to give whatever information is appropriate and leave it to the children to take it any further and possibly make contact. This is obviously a delicate area that has to be carefully worked out step by step.

Conclusion

There are many alternatives to the normal two parent family. Each one has a number of disadvantages, but may be able to offer better childcare than a dysfunctional two parent family. With careful planning and hard work it may be possible to limit the damage of family breakdown and some children manage to thrive in spite of all the adversity stacked against them.

In the long run the epidemic of family breakdown is likely to continue until our society gives parenting the high value it deserves and gives parents respect and recognition for doing the most important job of preparing the next generation to take charge of our world.

CHAPTER 6

FAMILY RELATIONSHIPS: QUESTIONS AND ANSWERS

Parents usually ask two types of questions when they have been given some advice. 'Yes but . . .' is what you are likely to say if you are not really convinced that the advice is correct and you can think of all kinds of reasons why you should not believe it. The other type of question is, 'What if . . .' asked by parents who think the advice seems sensible, but who can see some reasons why it might not work.

Yes But . . .

'I think babies bond to their mothers right from birth, rather than at about 6 months as you claim.'

There is some evidence that babies distinguish their own mother's milk from that of another mother and that from an early age they respond differently to their mother than to other people. But these are only the very first signs of the bonding process. Evidence of a real attachment isn't seen until a child starts to cling to the mother when being handed over to a stranger. This stage normally occurs around 5–7 months.

'My children were relieved when my husband and I decided to separate. I think that divorce is better than living with parents who hate each other.'

It isn't difficult to see why children are better off living in a home without arguments and bad feelings. However, they are likely to have seen and heard some shocking examples of poor relationships. Let's hope that they learn how to form good, lasting relationships in spite of what has happened. Most children need help with this.

If you decide to remarry or have a new relationship, the children may well find this more difficult to cope with than your divorce. They will need a lot of reassurance, affection, and attention during this period. At the same time it is important to be prepared to be quite firm about discipline and to avoid being overindulgent.

'My ex-husband insists on having weekly access even though it always upsets the children.'

It isn't unusual to have problems over access. The needs and wishes of the children should come first – after all, they are the innocent victims of the separation. Remember that children who maintain some contact with the absent parent do better in the long run.

If the children are old enough (8 years plus) to express a clear opinion it is best for this to be done face to face with the father. Alternatively they could write a letter, but this isn't as effective as direct contact.

If your ex-husband agrees, it may help to make the access shorter and less frequent. A common reason for children finding access distressing is that their parents are also distressed about it. You might find it helpful to think of access as being a bit like your child going to the dentist – it has to be done and they are better for it in the long run even if they become briefly upset at the time.

There are, however, limits to how much upset you and your children can be expected to cope with. If you feel that the upset is too much and your ex-husband has refused to change the access arrangements, it is a good idea to keep a diary of the effects of each access visit. The children's school may have some useful information on how they behave following their access visits. If it is impossible to negotiate a more satisfactory access for the children, then it may be necessary to involve solicitors and the courts, but this really should be as a last resort.

As a general rule, access visits shouldn't unsettle children for more than 36 hours after the visits are over.

'My son doesn't seem to get jealous at all.'

Children vary a lot in how strongly they experience jealousy. It depends on their personality, the way you have helped them deal with jealousy, and how secure and confident they feel. If your child shows no jealousy you should be pleased, but keep a look out for jealousy showing up in other less obvious ways.

'My children seem to argue and fight all the time.'

Sibling rivalry is the most likely cause of this, but you have to decide what level of arguing is acceptable in your family. Brothers and sisters often enjoy the fights, which can become almost reassuring for them because the fights are so familiar and predictable, in the same way that a habit like thumb sucking is comforting. Sometimes children fight because they see others being aggressive, for example on the TV or perhaps arguments between their parents. (See my book *Fighting, Teasing and Bullying* for further details.)

'Giving extra attention for jealousy is like rewarding bad behaviour.'

It is important to remember that jealous behaviour is the result of feeling distressed and not just being naughty. If you take no notice of a distressed child the behaviour will only get worse. However, exactly when you give the attention is critical. When the child is being resentful and jealous you should take as little notice as possible, apart from saying something that links the behaviour with the feeling of jealousy, and only give attention and comfort when your child is not aggressive.

'When should I give attention?'

Try to select your own time to give attention so that it is you who is in control rather than your child controlling you with difficult or unpleasant behaviour. It is also reasonable to give attention as soon as the jealous behaviour has finished, when you should make it clear that the reason that you are pleased is because they have stopped and they have managed to get their jealous feelings more under control.

'What should I say to my jealous child?'

Young children find it difficult to recognize their feelings and to tell one feeling from another. It is therefore a good idea to use any opportunity there is to help your child understand which emotion is which. However, when a child is behaving badly it is best not to say too much, partly because they won't take much notice and partly because they will enjoy having your attention. So when you see your child is behaving in a jealous way, it is worthwhile saying something simple like, 'I think you must be feeling jealous when you behave like that'.

'Why do girls get more jealous than boys?'

They don't. Girls are generally better than boys at using words to express their feelings, and boys become very good

at expressing their feelings through their behaviour while at the same time denying that they are upset!

'How can you tell that regression is due to jealousy?'

If your child regresses to babyish behaviour, all you know for certain is that the child is under stress. It is the timing of the regression that will give you the clue as to the most likely cause. But remember that jealousy is one of the most frequent causes of regression in young children.

'I think you should be fair and treat children equally.'

There is a difference between giving children *fair* treatment and giving them *equal* treatment. Of course it is right to try and be as fair as possible to a child, but because children have different individual needs it is unreasonable and in fact unfair to treat them equally.

Once your child understands that you take each individual's needs seriously, he or she will learn to accept that sometimes they have to miss out while the needs of another are met. The children will be reassured that when they have special needs you will do what you can to satisfy them – which is just another way of being fair!

'I don't agree with you so I will treat my children equally.'

It can't be done and in any case it is unfair. Some parents like their children to have the same bed-time, the same pocket money, and even the same presents. If one child has a birthday all the children will get a present. This system may work when children are very young, but they will soon start complaining, especially the eldest who will feel that they deserve more in return for the extra responsibility that they have.

'Surely children don't have to be taught to be caring and kind?'

A few children seem to be kind and thoughtful from a very young age, but most children are not. If you expect your child to be naturally caring, you are in for a disappointment, because most children are selfish and egotistic. This is why it is so important to teach children to be caring for others and not just hope for the best.

'You haven't said anything about the less common family arrangements.'

Apart from the alternatives to the two parent family outlined in Chapter 5 there are many different ways of creating a family home and bringing up children. The substitute parents may provide only part of the total parenting, but they can play a more significant role than the parents. Here are some of the variations of alternative parental care:

- **Grandparents**
- **Nanny**
- **Au-pair**
- **Extended family**
- **Boarding school**
- **Residential children's home**
- **Family groups**
- **The Kibbutz**

Each alternative form of childcare has its own advantages and disadvantages, but none of them is as satisfactory as a normal two parent family that is functioning well. You may be surprised to see au-pairs and boarding school listed as playing a parental role. They do in fact often play a more important parental role than the children's parents might care to believe.

Any of these arrangements can work reasonably well provided some basic rules are followed:

- **The quality of care is of a high standard.**
- **The child is clear about whom they belong to.**
- **The child is clear about who makes the final decisions about them.**
- **The parents and substitute carers communicate well with each other.**
- **There is general agreement on childcare issues.**
- **The time spent with the parents is happy and emotionally rewarding.**

Although the quality of care is all important, there is evidence that some children who have had very disturbed childcare can do surprisingly well as adults against all the odds. The most important factor that helps these children to do well is a continuing loving relationship. Good self esteem and a stable personality are also helpful, but neither is as crucial as long term supportive relationships.

'I think you are wrong to say that boarding school, au pairs, and nannies are all substitute parents.'

Children may spend a great deal of time with nannies, au pairs, and with the house parents at boarding school and these people often have a major and lasting effect on their lives. The amount of time spent with parents and the quality of the parent–child relationship will determine how much influence the parents will still have on their children.

What If . . .

'My ex wife deliberately sabotages my access to the children.'

This does happen sometimes, but often it is the distress of the separation that upsets the children. Every time they see you, they are reminded that their family has come to grief. If you are convinced that your wife is undermining your relationship with the children, it isn't any good having an argument about it. Negotiation and compromise is best, but if this isn't possible, it is best to go gently and try to build up trust again. Resorting to the courts costs money and human relationships and emotions don't respond well to coercion.

If you hang on in there and play for time, your children will eventually be old enough to express their own view. And if you have been able to maintain a good relationship with them, even if you have only seen them occasionally, you will be in a good position to continue the access with less bother than before.

'My daughter is highly strung and gets very jealous.'

'Highly strung' or 'sensitive' children feel all emotions, including jealousy, very strongly. You will probably find your daughter is hard work, because children with this type of personality are generally over-reactive right from birth, if not before!

Highly strung children don't need anything very different from other children in the way of help with jealousy. Just do all the normal things that you would do, only more so. And try and be calm yourself and avoid being swept along with the tide of your daughter's emotions.

'My children argue in spite of everything I do to stop them.'

The thing to watch out for is that you are not arguing with the children yourself when you try and stop them arguing, because this will only give them extra practice and an example to copy. Arguing soon becomes a habit and is then very difficult to stop. You will have to become very tough and determined if you want to put a stop to the arguments. Half-hearted measures won't work. The following approach should help:

- Nip all arguments in the bud.
- Teach them to share with each other.
- Teach them to care for each other.
- Don't join in the argument.
- If all else fails, separate them in different rooms.
- Keep at it until you are satisfied.

- **Start again immediately they slip back into their old ways.**

'My daughter is so jealous of the baby that she pulled his hair and hit him.'

Strong jealousy and resentment is so normal between a child and new baby that you should expect it and take precautions to avoid the physical manifestation of the jealousy. A child should not be left unsupervised with a baby until the baby is old enough to defend itself.

It is *your* responsibility to protect your baby, so don't blame your daughter. However, she must learn that being aggressive to the baby is totally unacceptable. The following ideas should help:

- **React immediately.**
- **Avoid the use of physical punishment.**
- **Use your words, your expression, and your tone of voice to leave no doubt exactly what you mean.**
- **Supervise your child closely at all times.**
- **Your daughter needs more lessons in sharing and being gentle.**

'My 6 year old son is still babyish, six months after his brother was born.'

Your son may still be under stress through jealousy which has not been dealt with. However, if there is no other obvious cause for the stress, you can assume that the regressed behaviour has become stuck as a habit. To help your child get out of the habit, try the following:

- **Take no notice of the babyish behaviour.**
- **Insist on grown-up behaviour before you do anything for your son.**

- Give praise whenever he is more grown-up.
- Give special privileges to encourage grown-up behaviour.
- It may help if you occasionally treat your son like a baby. Try something like an early bed time or wearing a bib – something that is a disadvantage. This should give your son such a surprise that he realizes that it is better to act his age. Keep it good fun, it isn't meant to be too serious!

'My 7 year old son started to wet himself after his sister was born.'

It isn't at all unusual for children to start wetting after the birth of a sibling. This regressive behaviour is more common in boys and in children who were slow in becoming completely dry in the first place. If the wetting doesn't stop in a week or two it is worthwhile helping your child to stop it before it becomes stuck as a habit. Here are some ideas:

- Get your son to take more responsibility for the wetting and involve him in the washing and changing of sheets.
- Your son could keep a diary to record any dry nights that he has.
- Dry nights should be praised as much as possible.
- Restricting fluids and lifting does not make a child become dry any quicker.
- Don't wait too long before getting professional help for the wetting if it is continuing. Older children can easily develop a sense of failure if they can't gain control of their own bladder. Don't be fobbed off with 'there is no need to worry – he will grow out of it soon'.

'My husband sulks when I do anything with the baby.'

It isn't at all unusual for a husband to be jealous of the attention his wife gives to the baby. It can be dealt with in much the same way as with a jealous child. The two most important things are:

- Involve your husband more in the care of the baby.
- Give him extra attention . . . poor chap!

JEALOUSY MAY CAUSE **SOME REGRESSIVE BEHAVIOUR** .... BUT IT WILL PASS....

'My wife seems to spend all her time looking after the baby.'

You had better give her some help then! Looking after a baby is a 'round the clock' job. You should arrange to give

your wife a complete rest if she seems to need it – and even
if she doesn't. You should also take your wife out or do
something special with her at least once a week. You both
need time together to keep your partnership going.

**'I have done everything you have suggested, but my
family still has serious relationship problems. I think
I need professional help for the whole family.'**

It is always difficult to know when is the right time to get
professional help with a child and/or family problem, and
even more difficult to know where to go and whom to ask.
Here are some suggestions if you feel it is necessary to get
some outside help:

- **Ask other parents and professionals what they
  know of the local services, but take what they say
  with a pinch of salt because individual opinions
  may be unreliable. One of the best informed people
  is likely to be your G.P.**
- **Voluntary groups for parents can be very supportive and give you an idea of how other people have
  coped. But they don't give professional advice,
  although they should be able to advise on how to
  get this type of help.**
- **There is a wide range range of professional groups
  who have specialized training and experience with
  family relationship problems. The difference between the various professions is confusing to say
  the least. One way round this problem is to ask your
  G.P. to refer the family to the local Child Psychiatry
  Service where it is usual for a range of different
  professionals to work closely together.**
- **Don't be put off a referral to a Consultant Child
  Psychiatrist; these are medically qualified doctors
  with a very broad training in the full range of child**

and family problems. They have special skills in helping any problem of emotions, behaviour, or relationships which seems to be getting out of control and out of proportion to what might be expected in the circumstances.

WHAT THE
RESEARCH SHOWS

The word family comes from the Latin *'familia'* meaning everyone who lives in the same household, including the servants. The Romans understood that there is more to a family than just blood relationships. Families come in all shapes and sizes, but there are distinct advantages to the 'normal' two natural parent family and their children. On the other hand, a dysfunctional two parent family may cause considerably more damage to children than a stable, caring alternative family arrangement. Nevertheless all families – however they are constituted – have a number of basic tasks to carry out, such as:

- **providing food, shelter, and protection from danger**
- **helping children adapt to life crises**
- **training children to be socially competent**
- **meeting the changing needs of development and maturation**
- **giving continuity of care throughout childhood**
- **ensuring children have positive self esteem**

Recent research has focused on the family as an interactive social system where each part affects each other part. The emotions, behaviour, and relationships of individuals in the family are therefore seen as the result of complex family interactions rather than being due to a single cause (Epstein and Bishop 1981).

The Birth of a Child

When the first child is born the single interpersonal relationship of the couple increases to three *dyadic* relationships and a *triadic* relationship. Some recent work has shown that this profoundly influences family interaction (Clarke-Stewart 1978). A well established marital bond plays a major part in maintaining the family unit through this period of change and potential crisis (Aldous 1978).

The birth of a second child leads to a dramatic increase in the number of possible relationships in the family. Dunn (1985) has reported great changes in the behaviour of the firstborn and in the quality of the interaction between the firstborn and the mother in the direction of more confrontation and naughtiness, but also in the child having to initiate more of the interactions with the mother.

These findings have the greatest relevance to clinical problems that arise with young children. For example, the birth of a second child may upset a previously satisfactory relationship between the mother and the first child and sow the seeds of a longstanding behaviour problem.

Separations from the Primary Caregiver

Separations from parents occur for many different reasons and numerous studies have shown an association between these events and disturbed behaviour and emotions. Dr John Bowlby (1980) considered that the primary affectional bond with the mother represented a prototype for all intimate human relationships, and damage to this primary relationship could result in difficulties for all subsequent relationships, particularly in the ability to sustain close relationships.

The general effects of separation are mainly due to innate attachment processes that occur in response to continuous loving care. Young children – particularly boys – who experience prolonged or repeated separations that occur in a critical and hostile environment are particularly vulnerable to disturbed behaviour (Rutter 1971).

In older children, separation anxiety may occur in the context of family over-involvement and relationships that are too close and protective. In some cases the interaction between an overprotective family and a child with separation anxiety can lead to school refusal (Hersov 1884).

Parental Divorce and Separation

Loss of a parent through separation following marital breakdown is now a common experience. About 1 in 3 marriages now end in separation and divorce, but not all of these involve children, so roughly 1 in 5 children will experience the separation of their parents before they are 16 years old.

Professor Judith Wallerstein and her colleagues (1980) in the USA, followed the progress of 131 children after their parents' divorce and found a high level of emotional distress and dysfunction. Fifty per cent of the children did not think that their family circumstances had improved after their parents' separation, presumably because marital discord usually involves children in repeated stressful situations over a long period:

- **Before the separation, children witness their parent's distress and anger**
- **Later there is the insecurity, sadness, and guilt of the separation, frequently followed by the difficulty of arranging access**

● **Finally children miss out yet again as their parents try to re-organize their own lives, which often involves establishing new relationships.**

Professor Mavis Hetherington (1982) has shown that there is a higher rate of psychiatric disorder in the children of divorce where the quarrelling and ill feeling between the parents continued so that the children were pawns in the marital conflict. This finding shows the importance of divorce conciliation counselling as a preventive measure.

In younger children there is a tendency for boys to show more disturbance than girls following the separation of their parents (Wallerstein and Kelly 1980). This sex difference is not so marked in older children and it is likely to be girls who show more overt disturbance in later adolescence. This is probably due to the differential vulnerability to stress of boys and girls at different ages. In general, the risk of psychiatric disorder in children who experience the separation of their parents is increased by at least twice the expected rate. Later on, children who come from a broken home have a higher than expected frequency of marital failure themselves in adult life.

The Death of a Parent

The changes in family structure and relationships that occur after the death of a parent are not dissimilar to those that occur after divorce. Bereaved children show a very similar range of emotional and behaviour disturbance to those following loss by separation and divorce (Raphael 1982). Young children show surprisingly little reaction to the death of their parent, especially if they experience continuity of satisfactory care. This is because children below the age of 8 years have difficulty grasping the finality of death. At 7–8 years of age children begin to understand concepts of individuality and of time. At this stage they no longer believe that the dead person has gone away like someone on holiday.

As with divorce, in the months following the loss of the parent there is an increased frequency of psychiatric disturbance which affects the majority of children initially, which then declines after a year (Van Eerdewegh et al 1982). Boys appear to be more vulnerable than girls to the death of a parent, particularly to the death of a father. This sensitivity of boys to the loss of a father has also been noted by Professor Rutter (1966) in a study of children of sick parents, some of whom later died.

There may be long term consequences for children who have experienced the death of a parent and there is some evidence that bereaved children have an increased risk of developing depression in adult life (Brown and Harris 1985). There is some dispute about whether this is directly due to the loss or the result of the many changes in family function and fortune. In the end it is the interaction of individual characteristics with past experience and present circumstances that determines the strength of the bereavement response.

Although the death of a parent is exceptionally traumatic for an older child, the amount of disturbed behaviour is generally much less severe and of shorter duration than is the case with children who have lost a parent by divorce. This is thought to be due to the continuing disturbance and disruption of relationships associated with divorce.

Parental Illness

Family relationships are altered by either physical or mental illness suffered by any family member. In the classic study of children of sick parents mentioned above, a strong link was found between parental mental illness and disturbance in their children (Rutter 1966). Much of this is due to general social factors and disturbed family relationships (e.g. Richman, Stevenson and Graham 1982). But there is also a tendency for some mental and physical illnesses to be experienced by a parent and a child in the same family, suggesting that genetic influences are also influential (Quinton and Rutter 1985).

Weintraub et al. (1986) investigated 243 children with parents suffering from affective disorder or schizophrenia. The children had a higher rate of deviant behaviour in a school setting than the control group. But some of the high risk children showed no significant disturbance, suggesting a high level of resilience.

The disturbance in children tends to be more marked if the parent has a neurotic rather than a psychotic illness and parents with personality disorder have a particularly adverse effect on their children (Rutter 1971). The critical factor appears to be the extent to which a child becomes involved and incorporated into their parent's illness.

No clear link has been established yet between any particular childhood disorder and the type of parental mental illness, but more recent research findings are tending to point to continuities in symptomatology between children and their parents (Cytryn et al. 1986). On the other hand no specific association between parental physical illness and childhood psychiatric illness has been found other than what might be expected to result from changes in family structure and function following the illness.

Family Size and Structure

Larger families (with more than 3 children) are associated with an increased risk of conduct disorder and delinquency (Rutter & Giller 1983). Large family size has also been linked with a slight increase in reading difficulty and a decrease in verbal ability (Rutter & Madge 1976), both of which are associated with anti-social behaviour (Rutter et al 1970).

The effect of the age gap between siblings has been reviewed by Wagner et al (1985). Research evidence suggests that academic achievement and social adjustment is better if the age gap is more than 4 years. This effect of higher achievement is also seen in only children. If there is a very close gap there is some evidence that firstborn children experience an increased frequency of dysthymic mood (i.e., morbid anxiety and despondency), and boys seem to be more vulnerable to a small age gap than girls.

Sibship position might be thought to be linked to a differential risk for psychiatric disorder, but in general there is little evidence to support this. However, eldest and only children have a tendency to be academically more successful (Rutter & Madge 1976), and eldest children are also slightly more prone to develop neurotic disorders. On the other hand youngest and only children may be more likely to experience separation anxiety (Rutter et al 1970).

Socio-Cultural Influences

Poverty is frequently associated with ill health, perinatal complications, over-crowding and delapidated housing, poor education, mental illness, criminality, one parent families, and unemployment. Each factor is in turn associated with the others and with an increased risk of disturbed family relationships (Rutter and Madge 1976).

There is strong evidence that adverse social influences not only tend to occur together, but also operate from a very early age. Wedge and Prosser (1973) identified a group of socially disadvantaged eleven year old children in the British National Child Development Study and found that they had a high rate of having young mothers, living in cramped conditions, and having had poor ante-natal care. The fathers were more likely to be off work and suffering from ill health and were less likely to have visited the child's school. Generally the disadvantaged children achieved less well academically, but a few children did unexpectedly well. Many children from a deprived background can be successful, provided there is consistent affection and predictable care. These findings give hope for intervention programmes (Elster et al 1987).

A recent study by Garcia Coll et al (1986) found that adolescent mothers experienced more life stress and interacted less with their infants than older mothers. It was concluded that the age, education, and socio-economic status of these young mothers led to less satisfactory child care and as a result their children were developmentally more delayed. The fathers of children born to young mothers are more likely to have a history of delinquency and to have experienced social and family adversity (Elster et al 1987). At the other end of the age range, there is no evidence that older parents affect the development of psychiatric disorder in their children. If anything, children of older parents have less disorder and achieve more academically.

Family Culture and Ethnicity

There is little doubt that ethnic origin and family culture make a significant impact on children's everyday life. What is less clear is the role that these influences play in the aetiology of psychiatric disorder. The importance of understanding the socio-cultural structure of ethnic minority groups has been highlighted by Gray and Cosgrove (1985). They looked at six minority groups in America and found that there were notable differences in the way responsibility was delegated to children. Issues of submission and dominance within the family system also varied from one group to another. It might be expected that children from mixed race marriages would have a higher rate of psychiatric disorder, but when socio-economic factors are controlled there is little evidence to support this view.

The link between emotional and behavioural problems and socio-cultural factors is unclear, but a person's age and sex seem to be important. For example, Earls and Richman (1980) found no difference in the rates of behavioural and emotional disturbance in 3–4 year old black children compared with white children, but black teenagers appear to have an increased rate of delinquency (Rutter and Giller 1983), and conduct disorder was more frequent in black girls compared with a matched group of white girls (Nicol 1971). These findings suggest that as children grow older, socio-cultural factors become more significant in their influence.

Atypical Families

Approximately 3 per cent of children are adopted and the evidence suggests that there is a small but definite increase in the prevalence of childhood psychiatric disorder in adopted children which cannot be explained simply by an increased awareness or a lower threshold for identifying problems (Hersov 1985).

Family structure and function may be altered by a parent in an unusual occupation or position. For example, it has been suggested that the children of undertakers suppress their emotions, the children of policemen have no friends and become delinquent, and the children of very prominent or successful parents may have a feeling of failure. Although this may be true in individual cases, there is insufficient research evidence to support this view.

It might be expected that parents with unusual sexual orientation, such as lesbian, homosexual, or transexual, would have children with an increased rate of disturbance. However, Green (1978) found no evidence of atypical sexual development in 37 children reared in families with homosexual or transsexual parents. Golombok et al (1983) came to similar conclusions when they compared children raised in lesbian households with children of single parents.

Protective Factors

It is important to remember that it is only a proportion of children who show an adverse outcome to family stresses. What is the difference between those children who suffer from family relationship problems and those that thrive in spite of them? One of the best studies to investigate this was carried out on the island of Kauai (Werner 1985). It was found that children brought up in small, well spaced families with a positive parent–child relationship in early childhood and additional caretakers besides their mother, did well in spite of experiencing poverty and hardship.

REFERENCES

Aldous, J., *Family Careers: Developmental Change in Families*. Wiley, New York (1978)

Bowlby, J., *Attachment and Loss*, Vols. 1–3, Hogarth Press, London (1980)

Brown, G.W., Harris, T.O., and Bifulco, A., Long term effects of early loss of a parent, *Depression in Young People: Developmental and Clinical Perspectives*, M. Rutter, C.E. Izard and P. Read (Eds), Guildford Press, New York, pp. 251–296 (1986)

Clarke-Stewart, K.A., And daddy makes three: the father's impact on mother and child, *Child Development*, 49, 446–478 (1978)

Dunn, J., The arrival of a sibling, *Longitudinal Studies in Child Psychology and Child Psychiatry*, A.R. Nicol (Ed.), Wiley, New York, pp. 15–31 (1985)

Earls, F. and Richman, N., The prevalence of behaviour problems in 3-year-old children of West Indian-born parents, *J. Child Psychol. Psychiat*, 21, 107–116 (1980)

Elster, A.B., Lamb M.E., Peters, L., Kahn, J., Tavere, J., Judicial involvement and conduct problems of fathers of infants born to adolescent mothers, *Paediatrics*, 79, 2:230–234 (1987)

Elster, A.B., Lamb, M.E., Tavere, J., Ralston, C.W., The medical and psychosocial impact of comprehensive care on adolescent pregnancy and parenthood, *JAMA*, 258, 9:1187–1192 (1987)

Epstein, N.B., Bishop, D.S. and Baldwin, L.M., Problem centred systems therapy of the family, *Handbook of Family Therapy*, A. Gurman and D. Kniskern (Eds), Brunner/Mazel, New York (1981)

Garcia Coll, C., Vohr, B.R., Hoffman, J., Oh, W., Maternal and environmental factors affecting outcome of infants of adolescent mothers. *Dev. Behav. Pediat.* 7, 4:230–236 (1986)

Golombok, S., Spencer, A. and Rutter, M., Children in lesbian and single parent households: psychosexual and psychiatric appraisal, *J. Child. Psychol. Psychiat.* 24, 551–572 (1983)

Gray, E., Cosgrove, J., Ethnocentric perception of child-rearing practices in protection services, *Child Abuse Neglect*, 9, 389–396 (1985)

Green, R., Sexual identity of 37 children raised by homosexual or transsexual parents, *Amer. J. Psychiat.* 135, 692–697 (1978)

Hetherington, E.M., Cox, M. and Cox, R., Effects of divorce on parents and children, *Non-traditional Families*, M.E. Lamb (Ed.), Lawrence Erlbaum, Hillside New Jersey, pp. 233–288 (1982)

Hersov, L.A., Adoption and fostering, *Child and Adolescent Psychiatry: Modern Approaches*, M. Rutter and L.A. Hersov (Eds) Blackwell Scientific Publications, London, pp. 101–117 (1985)

Nicol, A.R., Psychiatric disorder in children of Caribbean immigrants. *J. Child Psychol. Psychiat.* 12, 273–287 (1971)

Quinton, D. and Rutter, M., Parenting behaviour of mothers raised 'in care', *Longitudinal Studies in Child Psychology and Psychiatry*, A.R. Nicol (Ed.), Wiley, New York, pp. 157–201 (1985)

Raphael, B., The young child and the death of a parent, *The Place of Attachment in Human Behaviour*, C.M. Parks and J. Stevenson-Hinde (Eds), Basic Books, New York, pp. 131–150 (1982)

Richman, N., Stevenson, J. and Graham, P. J., *Pre-school to School: a Behavioural Study*, Academic Press, New York (1982)

Robertson, J. and Robertson, J., Young children in brief separations: a fresh look. *Psychoanal. Study Child.* 26, 262–315 (1971)

Rutter, M., Children of sick parents: an environmental and psychiatric study, *Institute of Psychiatry, Maudsley Monograph, No. 16*, Oxford University Press, London (1966)

Rutter, M., Parent–child separation: psychological effects on the children. *J. Child Psychol. Psychiat.* 12, 233–260 (1971)

Rutter, M. and Giller, H., *Juvenile Delinquency: Trends and Perspectives*, Guildford Press, New York (1983)

Rutter, M. and Madge, N., *Cycles of Disadvantage: A Review of Research*, Heinemann, London (1976)

Rutter, M., Tizard, J. and Whitmore, K. (Eds), *Education, Health and Behaviour*, Longmans, London (1970)

Van Eerdewegh, M.M., Bieri, M.D., Parrilla, R.H. and Clayton, P. J., The bereaved child, *Brit. J. Psychiat.* 140, 23–29 (1982)

Wagner, M.E., Schubert, H.J.P., Schubert, D.S.P., Effects of sibling spacing on intelligence, interfamilial relations, psychological characteristics and mental and physical health, *Advances in Child Development and Behaviour*, 19, 149–206 (1985)

Wallerstein, J.S. and Kelly, J.B., *Surviving the Breakup: How Children and Parents Cope with Divorce*, Grant McIntyre, London (1980)

Wedge, P. and Prosser, H., *Born to Fail?* Arrow Books in association with the National Children's Bureau, London (1973)

Weintraub, S., Winters, K.C. and Neale, J.M., Competence and vulnerability in children with an affectively disordered parent, *Depression in Young People: Developmental and Clinical Perspectives*, M. Rutter, C.E. Izard and

P.B. Read (Eds) Guildford Press, New York, pp. 205–220 (1986)

Werner, E.E., Stress and protective factors in children's lives, *Longitudinal Studies in Child Psychology and Child Psychiatry*, A.R. Nicol (Ed.), Wiley, Chichester, pp. 335–355 (1985)

FURTHER READING

Wallerstein, Judith and Blakeslee, Sandra, *Second Chances*, Corgi Books (1990).
The first book ever to outline the long term effects of divorce on children. A descriptive book, based on research work in the USA.

Rutter, Michael, and Madge, N., *Cycles of Disadvantage: A Review of Research*, Heinemann, London (1976).

Hetherington, E. M., Cox, M. and Cox, R., Effects of divorce on parents and children, *Non-traditional Families*, M.E. Lamb (Ed.), Lawrence Erlbaum, Hillside New Jersey, pp. 233–288 (1982).

Nicol, A. Rory (Ed.), *Longitudinal Studies in Child Psychology and Child Psychiatry*, Wiley, New York, pp. 15–31 (1985).

Goldstein, Joseph, Freud, Anna, and Solnit, Albert, *Beyond the Best Interests of the Child*, Free Press, New York (1973).

Rutter, Michael (Ed.)., *Scientific Foundations of Developmental Psychiatry*, Heinemann, London (1980).

INDEX